Questions and Answers

GEOGRAPHY

Mike Clinch Examiner
Graham Woosnam Chief Examiner

SERIES EDITOR: BOB McDUELL

Letts
EDUCATIONAL

Contents

HOW TO USE THIS BOOK	1
THE IMPORTANCE OF USING QUESTIONS FOR REVISION	1
TYPES OF EXAMINATION QUESTION	2
EXAMINATION TECHNIQUE	2
COMMAND WORDS	3

QUESTIONS AND REVISION SUMMARIES

1 The water cycle and rivers and their valleys	4
2 Coasts	8
3 Weathering and glaciation	12
4 Weather and climate	16
5 Population and resources	23
6 The urban world	26
7 Urbanisation	30
8 Agriculture	34
9 Manufacturing industry	37
10 Tourism and leisure	40
11 Employment structures in developed and developing countries (MEDCs and LEDCs)	45
12 Mock examination paper	52

ANSWERS	57

Introduction

HOW TO USE THIS BOOK

The aim of the *Questions and Answers* series is to provide you with help to do as well as possible in your exams at GCSE at both Foundation and Higher levels or, in Scotland, at General and Credit levels. This book is based on the idea that an experienced Examiner can give, through examination questions, sample answers and advice, the help students need to secure success and improve their grades.

This *Questions and Answers* series is designed to provide:

- Introductory advice on the different types of questions and how to answer them to maximise your marks.
- Information about the **assessment objectives**, which includes understanding and the application of knowledge, that will be tested in the examinations. The *Questions and Answers* series is intended to develop these skills by showing you how marks are allocated.
- **Revision summaries** to remind you of the topics you will need to have revised in order to answer examination questions.
- Many examples of **examination questions**, arranged by topic, with spaces for you to fill in your answers, just as on an examination paper. Only try the questions once you have revised a topic thoroughly. Read the Revision Summary before attempting the questions to double-check you know the topic. It is best not to consult the answers before trying the questions.
- **Sample answers** to all of the questions.
- **Advice from Examiners**. By using the experience of actual Chief Examiners we are able to give advice on how you can improve your answers and avoid the most common mistakes.

THE IMPORTANCE OF USING QUESTIONS FOR REVISION

Past examination questions play an important part in revising for examinations. However, it is important not to start practising questions too early. Nothing can be more disheartening than trying to do a question which you do not understand because you have not mastered the topic. Therefore, it is important to have studied a topic thoroughly before attempting any questions on it.

How can past examination questions provide a way of preparing for the examination? It is unlikely that any question you try will appear in exactly the same form on the papers you are going to take. However, the Examiner is restricted on what can be set because the questions must sample the whole syllabus and test certain key ideas. The number of totally original questions that can be set on any part of the syllabus is very limited and so similar ideas occur over and over again. It certainly will help you if the question you are trying to answer in an examination is familiar and you know you have done similar questions before. This is a great boost for your confidence and confidence is what is required for examination success.

Practising examination questions will also highlight weaknesses in your knowledge and understanding. Thus revision can be targeted more accurately. It will also indicate which sorts of questions you can do well and which, if there is a choice of questions, you should avoid.

Attempting past questions will get you used to the type of language used in questions.

Finally, having access to answers, as you do in this book, will enable you to see clearly what is required by the Examiner, how best to answer each question, and the amount of detail required. Attention to detail is a key aspect of achieving success at GCSE.

Introduction

TYPES OF EXAMINATION QUESTION

All questions in geography examinations are there for a purpose: to find out how well you can recall factual data, how well you understand their significance and whether you can use a range of geographical skills.

Usually, a question tests the above using one particular theme or key idea from the syllabus, though sometimes, as you will discover in this book, questions may jump from one theme to another in an attempt to ensure that all parts of the syllabus are tested.

Questions can vary in their form very widely. They range from, at one extreme, **multiple choice questions** to, at the other extreme, an **open essay**-type question. In GCSE Geography most questions are of an intermediate **structured type**.

Only a few syllabuses still set multiple choice questions. This type of question tends to test factual recall or the understanding of simple facts only, and not a candidate's ability to develop and sustain an argument. Open essay-type questions are also rare at GCSE. They aim at high level qualities such as analysis, synthesis and evaluation. Thus, if they occur at GCSE it will be in the Higher tier papers or comparable Scottish examination.

Structured questions are the norm in most GCSE examinations. Questions of this type are broken up into small parts (a), (b), (c) and sometimes (d). These three or four sub-questions may be further broken down into (i), (ii), (iii) etc. Most of the questions in this book are of this kind. Each of the sub-questions will have the mark allocation alongside.

Most structured GCSE Geography questions are rich in resources – maps, photographs, graphs, diagrams, newspaper extracts etc. They are there to trigger off ideas in your mind and to provide you with information that you can make use of in your responses. Hence, these questions are often referred to as data response questions. Only small parts of these questions may demand straight factual recall.

Normally, there is an incline of difficulty in these questions; that is, the question gets progressively more difficult as one proceeds through it. The early parts of the question may seek short answers of a factual nature, or may test simple skills. The later parts of the question may be more searching, with explanation or discussion required. In some syllabuses, the final part may concentrate on a case study that you will be expected to have made. Do not be too worried if half-way through a question you have difficulty in answering. You personally may find the final sub-question less demanding. If you are sitting the Higher tier paper, you may not have the easier 'factual recall section'. You will have more of the free response-type question, which is aimed at testing your higher levels of ability.

EXAMINATION TECHNIQUE

There are certain fundamental features about examinations which every year are overlooked by some candidates, to their cost. So, however obvious they may appear, it will do you no harm to think about them now.

- You will be sitting a differentiated examination, i.e. an examination where you may sit a 'less difficult' or 'more difficult' paper. Make sure that you receive and answer the appropriate one.

- Be aware of the nature of the paper. Are all the questions compulsory or do you have to make a choice? If they are all compulsory, you may wish to tackle the questions you feel best prepared for first, or you may like to answer the questions in order; there are no hard and fast rules.

- If there is a choice of questions to be made, it is vital that you make the choice that is **right** for you. Do not be lured into choosing a question because it starts with an appealing

Introduction

photograph and diagram or because you find the first sub-question easy. The question might change course and become very difficult for you. In short, read all the questions through carefully before you make your choice.

- Note the mark award in the margin of the question and, if included, the number of lines the examiner has allowed you to write on. This is a good guide to the depth of answer required. There is not much sense in writing at length or continuing the answer on extension pages if the question awards only one or two marks.

- Most geography examinations encourage you to draw sketch maps or diagrams in some of your answers. Some questions actually demand it. If this is the case, ensure that you do so, otherwise you will lose marks. Bear in mind that a well-drawn, labelled sketch map or diagram can state in quite a small space much more than an equal amount of writing. There are examples of sketch maps and diagrams in this book for you to study.

- In your studies in geography you will have learned not only facts and skills but also acquired a range of ideas and concepts. An Examiner may wish to test your understanding of these, perhaps in a context that is unfamiliar to you. For example, you may have studied the issue of overpopulation in north-east Brazil. The Examiner may use the Nile Valley or somewhere else in the world, on which to base the question. Do not let the location deter you from focusing on, in this case, the concept of overpopulation.

- In any examination you must be aware of the pressure of time. Work out the amount of time you have for each question if you spend the same amount on each. It is natural that if you feel supremely 'on top' of one question you may wish to spend a little longer on this than the other questions – but be careful! You must leave enough time to make a worthwhile attempt at your last question. Not answering a question, or even just a sizeable part of it, can all too easily cost you a grade.

COMMAND WORDS

Finally, pay attention to the command word used in each question.

Name, **state**, **list** and sometimes **give**, are words used when the Examiner wants simple, short answers. **Give reasons for** is different. This is similar to **explain.**

Define merely asks for a definition, i.e. the meaning of a word. This should be easy but this is not always the case – simple words can be taken for granted, e.g. define wind.

Describe asks for a longer answer than state or name. You are expected to give details about what is shown without attempting an explanation. This differs from **explain** where you should attempt to make something clear by giving reasons for it. Clearly describing a meander is very different from explaining its existence.

Outline used as a command word is similar to describe, but implies that you pick out the main points in a topic or process in a succinct way. It does **not** mean that you draw an outline map.

Suggest implies that there is more than one answer or more than one approach possible. You state what you feel is appropriate.

Compare (and maybe **contrast**) asks you to think in a comparative manner. You should not write two separate accounts. If asked to compare housing in an outer suburb with that in an inner city suburb, the comparative '**er**' and words like '**more**' or '**less**' will occur. For example, housing in outer suburbs is dear**er**, is larg**er**, is **more** spread out than housing in the inner city. There is much **less** garden space in inner city housing.

Discuss is a more demanding command word. It expects the candidate to describe and explain and to give both sides of the argument.

Analyse is not used very often at GCSE level. It means to examine a topic in detail, to get down to the structure and essence of the matter.

1 The water cycle and rivers and their valleys

REVISION SUMMARY

The hydrological or water cycle is the term used to describe the progression of water falling from the atmosphere to the Earth as precipitation, eventually returning to the atmosphere through the processes of evaporation and transpiration. The precipitation which falls onto the land surface, and which is not evaporated, runs over the surface through rivers and back to the sea. The diagram below summarises the water cycle.

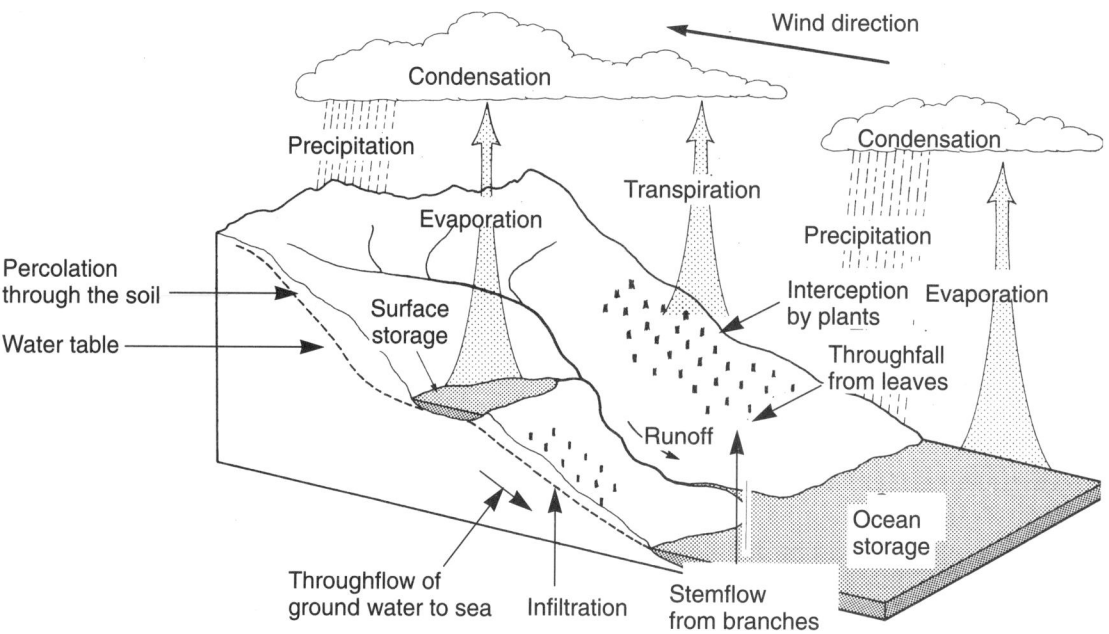

The water cycle

A **drainage basin** is an area of land drained by one river system (a river and its tributaries). The basin's limit is marked by higher land which separates it from neighbouring drainage basins. This limit is called a **watershed**.

A river system and water stored in the ground depend for their existence on precipitation. This is the drainage basin's **input**. Water moving out of the basin through the river and evaporation/transpiration is the basin's **output**. Within the basin, water may be held for a long time in lakes, the soil, vegetation and the ground. This is the basin's **storage**.

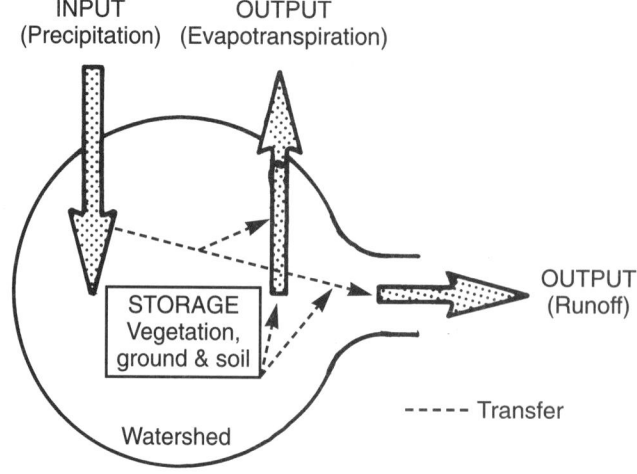

The drainage basin as a system

Rivers and streams flowing through a river basin possess energy. The amount of energy varies according to the river volume (the bigger the volume, the greater the energy), the shape of the river

The water cycle and rivers and their valleys

channel and the river gradient. This energy allows rivers to do work. They erode material from the land surface, carry this material (**load**) downstream, then deposit it in their lower courses or in the sea.

There are three main processes of erosion:

(i) **corrasion** (sometimes called abrasion) – the wearing away of the bed and banks of a river through the impacting of the river's load against them;
(ii) **hydraulic action** – the very force of water prising rocks away;
(iii) **corrosion** – the dissolving and removal in solution of some rocks, e.g. limestone, over which the river flows.

Most erosion takes place during times of flood.

Landforms

The following landforms are typical of most rivers in the British Isles.

A In its upper section, a river erodes predominantly vertically so the valley will be deeper than it is wide giving a **V-shaped cross-section**. The river gradient (long profile) is steep, with **waterfalls** where it crosses rocks of different resistance, while the river's course is winding creating **interlocking spurs**.

B In its middle (valley) section the valley sides are still steep, but the valley floor is wider as the river erodes laterally as well as vertically. This flat floor (or **flood plain**) will have been created by river **meanders** as they migrate downstream. This flat land is flooded periodically. During such floods rivers deposit their load (**alluvium**), keeping the flood plain fertile.

A meander is a loop in the river's course. Water flows faster around the outside of the loop than on the inside. Consequently, erosion (through corrasion and hydraulic action) leads to undercutting of the river banks on the outside of the bend. Here slopes may be steep giving **river cliffs**. On the inside there is deposition of silt and the gradient here is gentle. This is called a **slip off slope**.

C Further downstream the river's energy becomes less and erosion is more than balanced by deposition. Here the flood plain is wide. Meanders may be less sinuous having been cut through by the river in times of flood. This will have created **oxbow lakes** (see Question 1). River banks may be quite high (**levees**). When entering the sea or a lake the river water's velocity is checked and its load is deposited. This may create a **delta**. If the level of the sea has risen in the recent past an **estuary** will be formed.

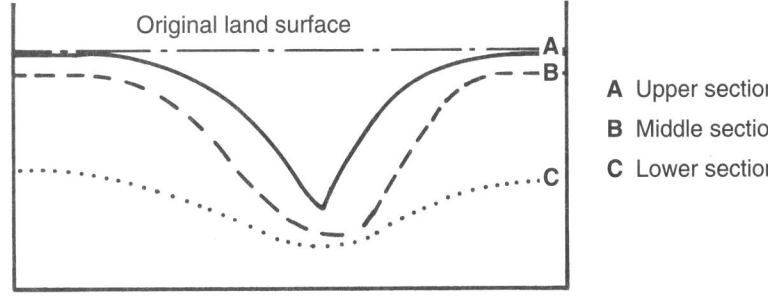

A Upper section
B Middle section
C Lower section

Three typical cross-sections of a river valley

Humans use rivers for a variety of purposes:
- for the transport of goods, e.g. barges on the river Rhine;
- as clearly marked boundary lines, e.g. ten states of the USA use the Mississippi;
- as sources of drinking and irrigation water and of hydroelectric power. For these uses the river has to be dammed and a reservoir created. A narrow damming point, impermeable rock, a large water storage area, a regular supply of water and a sparse population to minimise the risk of pollution, are all desirable.

> **REVISION SUMMARY**
>
> If you need to revise this subject more thoroughly, see the relevant topics in the *Letts* GCSE *Geography Study Guide*.

1 The water cycle and rivers and their valleys

QUESTIONS

1 (a) Study Fig. 1 below, which gives information about the hydrological (water) cycle.

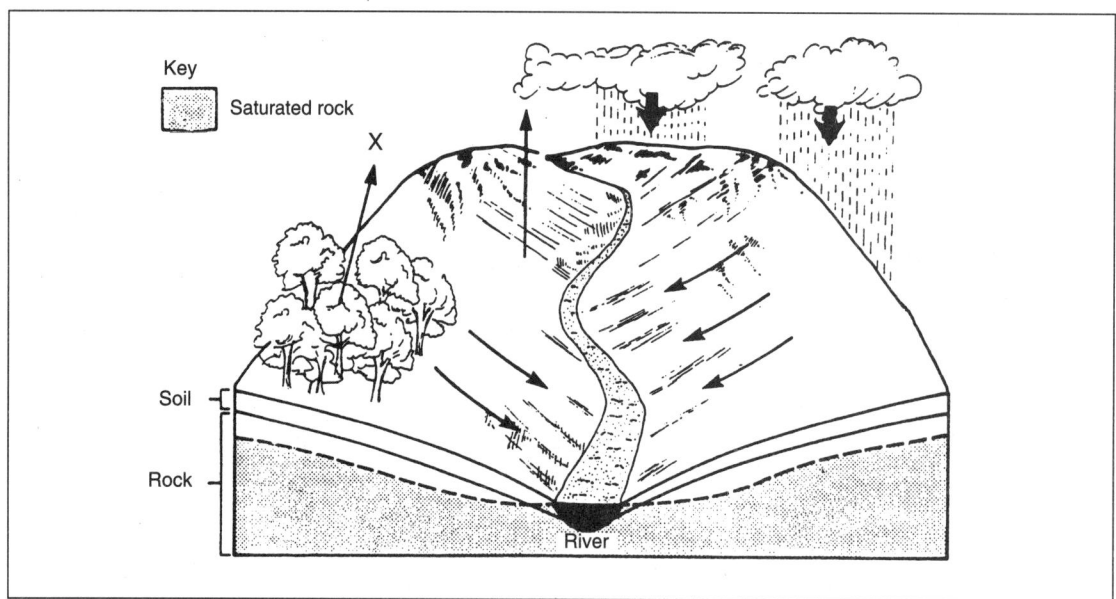

Fig. 1

   (i) Listed below are some of the processes in the hydrological cycle.

   Evaporation   Runoff   Precipitation   Condensation

   Show these processes in the correct order on the diagram below. The first process, evaporation, has been done for you. (1)

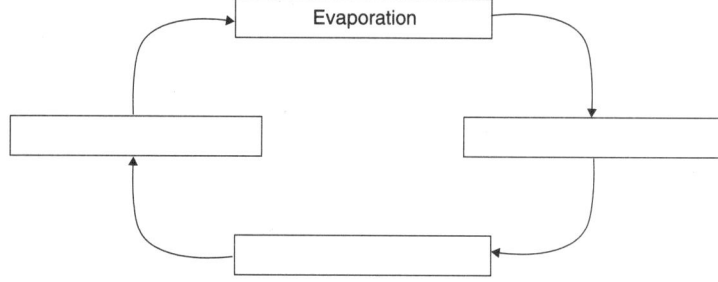

   (ii) Name the process which is taking place at X on Fig.1. (1)

   (iii) Why will the process you have named in (a) (ii) be greater in summer than in winter? (1)

   (iv) What is the name given to the upper level of saturation of soil and rock shown by the pecked line (— — — —) on Fig.1? (1)

(b) Study the OS map extract of Keswick on page 50, scale 1:50 000, showing part of the Lake District in north-west England.

   (i) Name the river feature found at map reference 256235. (1)

   (ii) Describe the main features of the River Derwent between its exit from Derwent Water (255232) and the western edge of the map extract (240263). (3)

The water cycle and rivers and their valleys

(iii) **Using map evidence only**, name and describe the physical feature formed by the River Derwent at the southern end of Derwent Water. The feature is found to the east of Great Bay. (3)

(iv) Explain how the feature you have described in (b) (iii) may have been formed by the work of the river. (3)

(c) River valleys, such as the one shown on the OS map extract, often suffer from flooding.

(i) Give **two** reasons why flooding takes place in river valleys. (2)

(ii) How may people change the shape of the channel and banks of a river to prevent flooding in the future? (2)

(d) Study Fig. 2, below, which shows part of a river valley.

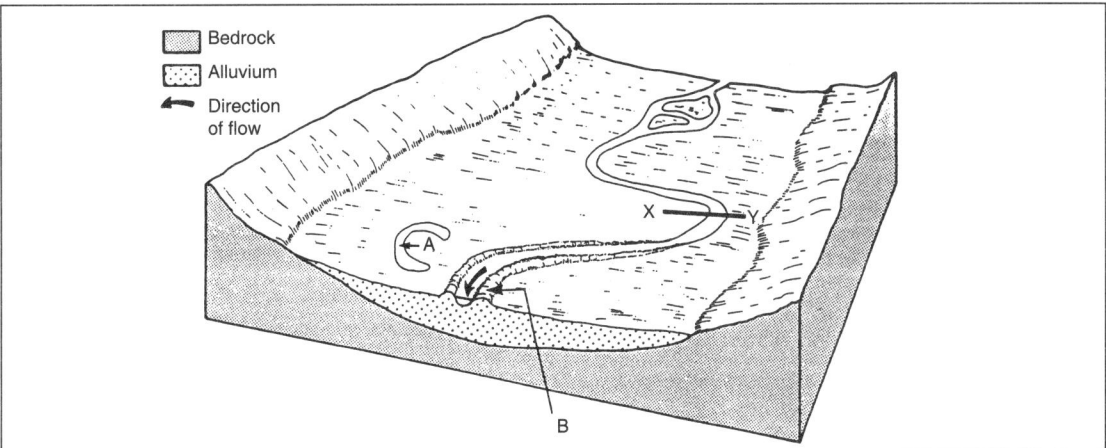

Fig. 2

(i) Name **one** of the physical features labelled A or B. (1)

(ii) Draw a cross-section along the line X–Y to show the shape of the river's channel. Use the grid provided below. On your section, mark with the letter M the position of the river's maximum speed. (2)

Fig. 2b

(iii) Choose **either** feature A or feature B. Explain how the feature you have chosen may have been formed by the river processes. (4)

MEG 1993

2 Coasts

REVISION SUMMARY

Probably the most important agents shaping the coastline are waves, which operate between high and low tide levels. They get their energy from the wind. The stronger the wind and the greater the distance it blows over the sea (its fetch), the higher the wave. Waves are surges of energy through the water. The water itself does not move forward until the wave reaches the coast and begins to break. Waves reaching the coast are often classified as **destructive** or **constructive**. Destructive waves plunge suddenly. Much of their water flows back down the beach (**backwash**) taking material with it, i.e. they erode. They are quite frequent (10–14 per minute). Constructive waves are linked with more gently shelving shores. Their water tends to move up the beach (**swash**) taking material with it, i.e. they build up beaches. They are less frequent (6–8 per minute).

Destructive waves erode the coast by:

- **hydraulic action** – two subdivisions exist: **(i) wave pounding**, waves may pound the rock at 30 tonnes per square metre, and **(ii) hydraulic pressure**, where air in cracks in the rock is alternately compressed and expanded. Both these processes weaken the rock.
- **corrasion (abrasion)** – cliffs are worn away by pebbles etc. being hurled at them by waves.
- **solution** – certain rocks, e.g. limestone, are soluble in sea water.
- At the same time material carried by the sea is being worn by **attrition**.

The rate of erosion and the nature of the landforms created also depends on the nature and the structure of the rocks making up the coastline. Resistant rocks (e.g. granite and hard sandstones) stand out as headlands. Less resistant rocks (e.g. clays and shales) are eroded more quickly to form bays. Hence, where a coastline consists of alternating bands of hard and soft rocks, a headland and bay coastline will result. Rocks which have been faulted or contain many joints are also susceptible to erosion.

Erosion landforms include **cliffs** and **wave cut platforms**, **caves**, **arches**, **stacks** and **bays**, though the latter may later become areas of deposition. Destructive waves attacking the land create a notch which, over time, enlarges to create a steep slope called a cliff. The cliff is then undercut by the waves, through the processes of erosion outlined above. The resultant overhang collapses and the cliff face retreats. As it retreats, the wave cut platform at its base widens. Eventually it becomes so wide that the waves lose their energy before reaching the cliff base. The cliff then becomes less steep as it is attacked by subaerial agents.

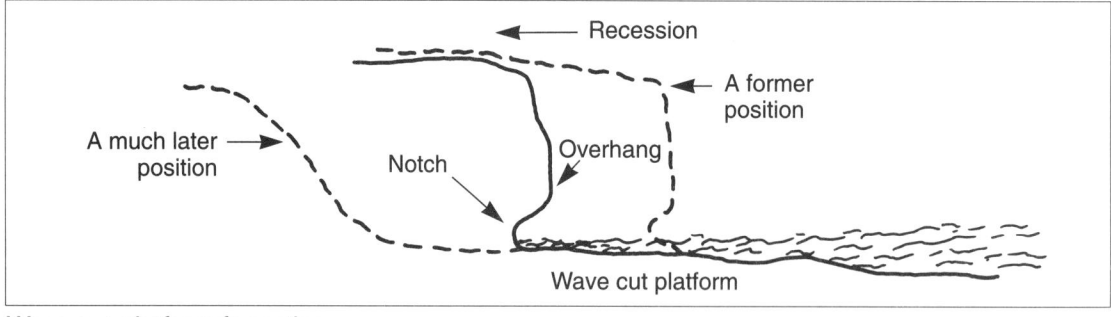

Wave cut platform formation

Cliffs that are made up of rocks that dip seawards tend to be eroded more quickly than those whose rocks dip landwards. If cliffs on a headland are faulted, it is likely that a cave will form at the fault. This may penetrate right through the headland to create an arch. This will eventually collapse to create a stack, then a stump.

Eroded material is moved along a coast by **longshore drift** and creates features of deposition elsewhere – usually where the coastline has a gentle gradient and the waves are constructive. The material moved may be added to by material washed down by rivers. Longshore drift occurs because most waves approach the shore obliquely and, therefore, carry material along in a zigzag fashion, as shown in the diagram on page 9.

Coasts 2

REVISION SUMMARY

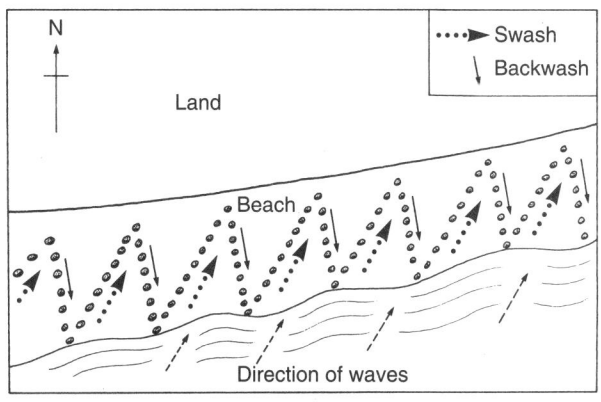

Longshore drift

Landforms created by the deposition of material include: **beaches**, **spits**, **mud flats** and **deltas**. A beach is a stretch of sand/shingle/pebbles deposited between HWM and LWM along a coast. It is a consequence of constructive waves and longshore drift. Beaches occur where the input of material exceeds depletion. Bay head beaches are usually much smaller and result from waves losing energy within a bay.

If a beach coastline changes direction, the deposited material may carry on being deposited in a straight line out to sea. This narrow finger of sand/shingle is called a spit and may become several kilometres long. Sand may pile up, through the action of the wind, into dunes. They may become fixed by marram grass. Eventually, the end of the spit may swing around to form a 'hook'. Behind the spit in the almost calm waters, mud and silt will settle and create a salt marsh.

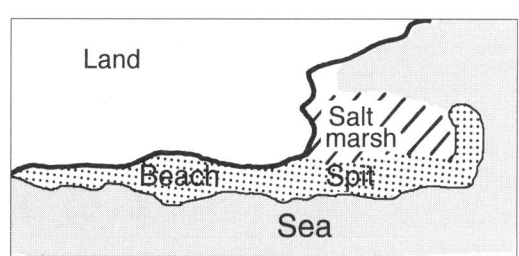

Spit formation

Deltas can occur where rivers enter the sea (or a lake). The river's velocity is abruptly checked, so it loses its energy and drops its load. Reaction to sea water helps deposition, as clay particles will cohere more readily. Deposition is also helped if the sea has low or no tides. Hence, deltas are common at the mouths of rivers entering the Mediterranean sea, e.g. Nile, Rhône. Deltas provide areas of flat, often fertile, land.

If sea level has risen over recent geological time, relative to the land, the coastline will become irregular with inlets at the mouths of rivers. These are **estuaries**. If the 'drowning' by the sea is greater, the whole lower course of a number of river valleys may be flooded permanently, creating a **ria** coastline.

Coastal areas are increasingly affected by human activities. In an attempt to preserve their beaches some resorts build artificial barriers (groynes) at right angles to the shore to prevent the longshore drift of sand. This may cause beaches further along the coast to disappear as their sand supply diminishes and also any cliffs there to suffer greater erosion. Removal of sand supply and shingle from the sea bed some distance out to sea for the building industry is also thought to be depleting beaches and thereby increasing erosion. Industrial and tourist developments on estuaries and small bays may destroy the breeding grounds of migrating birds. Wildlife and sometimes human life also suffers because of pollution. Sewage is a major pollution problem along the coasts of many developed countries. Not only does it contaminate beaches, it also takes oxygen from the sea, harming marine life. Pollution from farmland fertilisers, polluted water from estuarine industries and oil from ships washing out their tanks are other pollutants which mar coastal environments.

If you need to revise this subject more thoroughly, see the relevant topics in the *Letts GCSE Geography Study Guide.*

2 Coasts

QUESTIONS

1 Study Fig. 1, a sketch map of the Pegwell Bay area in East Kent, and the aerial photograph below which shows part of the same area.

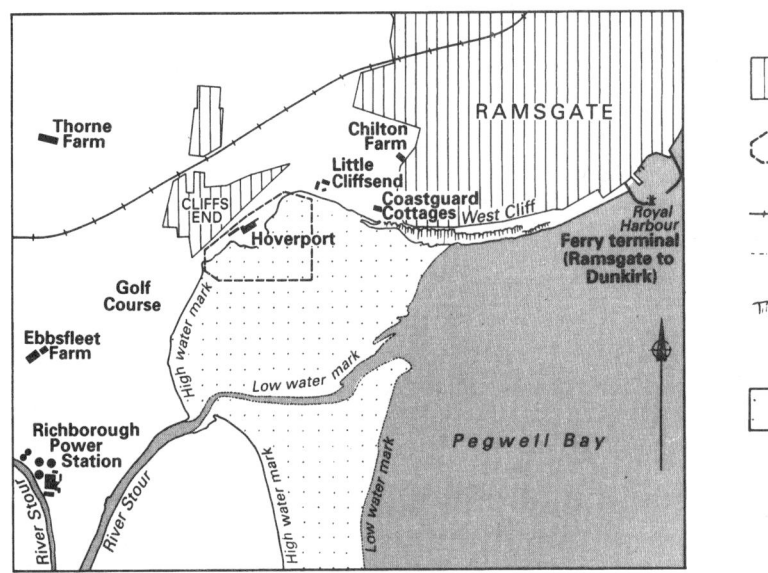

Fig. 1 Pegwell Bay

A part of Pegwell Bay

By courtesy of Aerofilms

Coasts 2

QUESTIONS

(a) (i) Name the features X and Y on the photograph.

    (ii) Using evidence from the map and the photograph state **four** other uses that are made of this coastal area.

    (iii) State **one** piece of evidence which suggests that the photograph was taken at high tide. (7)

(b) Study Fig. 1 and Fig. 2, which provide details of major development proposals for the area identified on the map and the photograph.

DEVELOPMENT PROPOSALS FOR PEGWELL BAY		
Overall aim	– To create a unique coastal environment.	
Means	– By creating a shallow recreational basin protected by a ring of artificial islands. These islands would create a new wildlife sanctuary while the existing beach area will be retained. The site is planned as an all weather recreation/leisure and small conference complex, a waterside residential community and dinghy marina with supporting retail outlets. The residential units will be developed for the personal and business tourist markets, second and permanent home buyers. The recreational/leisure facilities will be available to the residents and to the general public on a membership basis.	

Site details	– Residential units
	    Retail units
	    Recreation/leisure
	    Artificial basin
	    Artificial islands
	    Dinghy berths
		– Approx 400
		 – Approx 5,000 sq. ft.
		 – 7.5 acres
		 – Approx 70 acres
		 – Approx 3 acres+
		 – 100+

Fig. 2

    (i) Give **two** facts which show that the developers are concerned about the natural environment of the area.

    (ii) What will need to be demolished before the development can take place?

    (iii) Suggest why it is necessary to construct the artificial islands.

    (iv) Suggest **two** reasons why it is proposed to create a shallow recreational basin when a large bay already exists. (6)

(c) The residents of Cliffs End have divided opinions about the scheme.

    (i) Suggest **three** reasons why many are likely to support the scheme.

    (ii) Suggest **one** possible objection they might have. (4)

(d) Pollution is an increasing problem along coastlines. For an area you have studied where this problem is or has been particularly serious:

    (i) Name the area and describe the type(s) of pollution involved.

    (ii) Explain what measures are being taken or were needed to reduce the level of pollution. (8)

LONDON 1993

3 Weathering and glaciation

REVISION SUMMARY

Weathering

Weathering is the break-up of rock *in situ* on the surface of the land through the action of atmospheric and biological agents. It is the first stage in soil formation and is an essential preliminary to erosion by rivers, ice, the sea and wind. There are three main types of weathering.

Physical (or mechanical) weathering: this breaks up the rock into smaller and smaller pieces, but there is no chemical change. It is caused by: (i) large temperature changes within a rock and/or (ii) by the alternate freezing and thawing of water, both causing stresses within the rocks so that they fracture. Process (ii) is often called frost shattering. The products of such weathering are angular in shape and may, under gravity, slip down slopes, collecting at the bottom as a scree slope. Physical weathering is common in the cooler and drier parts of the world.

Chemical weathering: this causes the rotting of rocks, which are decomposed by carbon dioxide and other organic acids. Such weathering is more common in the warmer and wetter parts of the world. Soluble rocks are more prone to this type of weathering. Much of the weathered material is subsequently removed in solution. The role of chemical weathering has become more significant during this century as human beings have released more chemicals into the atmosphere. Some of these return to the ground as acid rain, speeding up chemical weathering.

Biological weathering: this describes those processes where plant roots prise open rocks (physical) and humic acids from vegetation and bacteria attack the rocks (chemical).

It is important to realise that all three types of weathering usually act together.

Glaciation

There have been Ice Ages, i.e. periods when ice covered significant portions of the Earth's surface, regularly during the Earth's history. Just 18 000 years ago much of the British Isles was covered by ice. During these cold phases, snow which fell in winter gradually lasted longer and longer on the ground until it became permanent. Snow which fell in hollows became deeper until the lower layers of snow turned to ice through compression. Ice collected high up in valleys and then moved down them as glaciers. Sometimes these glaciers, reaching lowland areas, merged to form ice sheets.

Ice moving downhill is able to erode, using materials made available to it by earlier weathering and river action. The material it carries is called moraine (see diagram for further details).

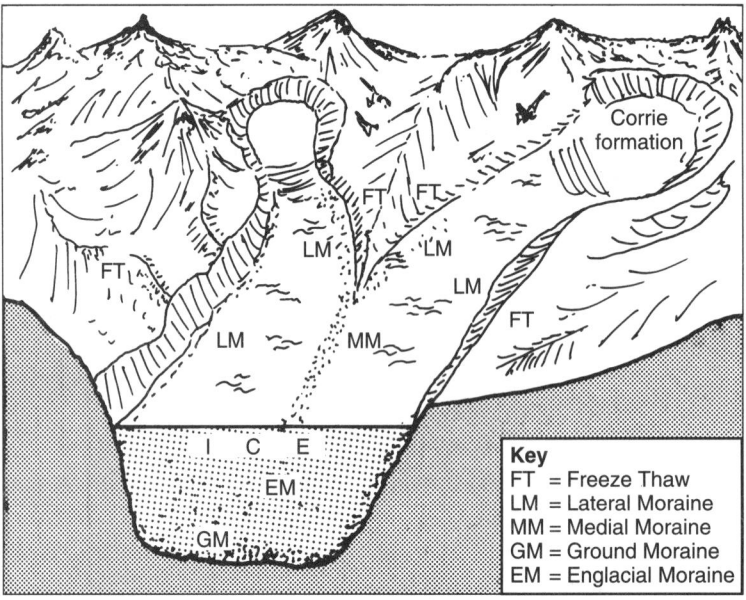

Types of moraine

Weathering and glaciation 3

REVISION SUMMARY

The two main processes of ice erosion are **abrasion** and **plucking**. Abrasion is the grinding away and polishing of rock on the valley floor and sides by the moraine (load) sticking out of the moving glacier. Near the base and sides of the glacier ice melts into and refreezes around jointed or protruding rock and, as the glacier then moves, it pulls these rocks away. This is plucking. Above the glacier, **freeze thaw** will be active giving the supraglacial landscape a jagged appearance and providing the glacier with a constant supply of material.

Features of glacial erosion include glacial valleys or troughs and above them **corries** (or cirques), **arêtes**, **pyramidal peaks** and **hanging valleys**. **Glaciated valleys** were once river valleys. These were deepened and widened by the processes mentioned above to become **U-shaped troughs**. Corries were hillside hollows which were enlarged and deepened by ice. They consequently became lake-filled. Arêtes are the narrow ridges between the back walls of corries, while a pyramidal peak marks the junction of four corries.

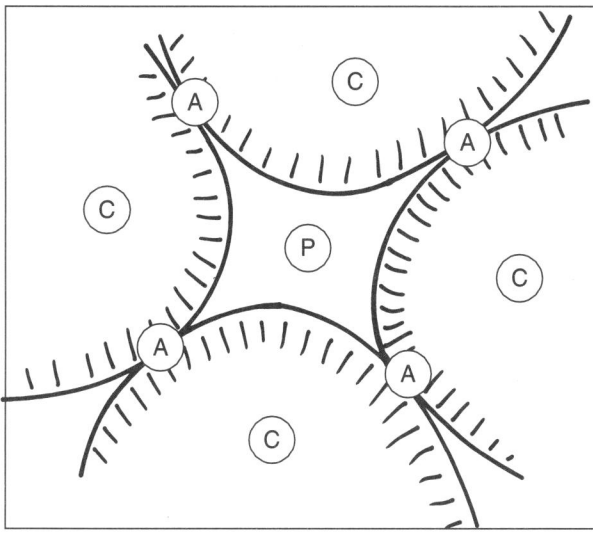

Hanging valleys are tributary valleys, with floors which are now found well above the main valley. They were deepened much less by the smaller, tributary glaciers occupying them, than was the main valley by its larger glacier. The drops between the two valley floors are now frequently marked by waterfalls.

Where valley glaciers or ice sheets move into lowlands, the moraine they carry will be deposited as they melt (ground moraine or boulder clay). If deposition takes place at the front of a stationary ice sheet or glacier (from melting streams) sometimes a long, ridge-like **terminal moraine** may form. Such moraines at the end of a valley glacier may in effect deepen a glacially eroded hollow and create or enlarge a ribbon lake.

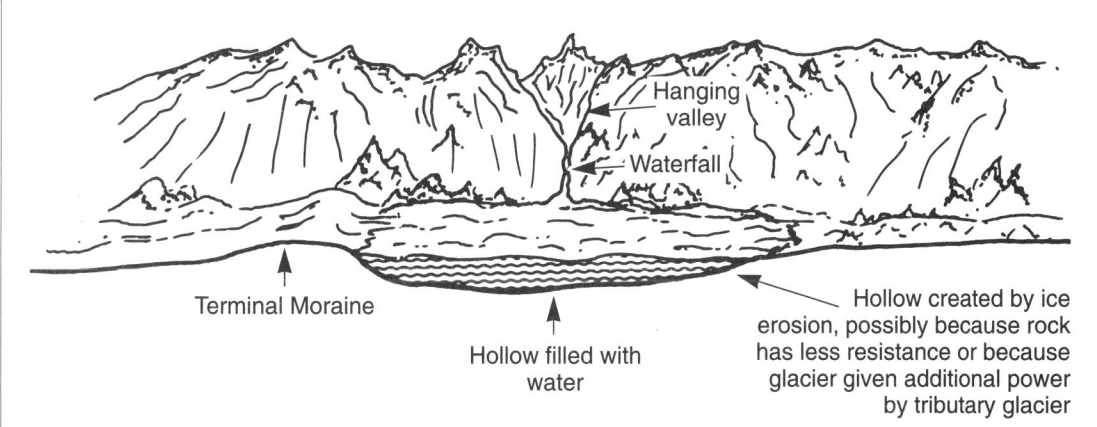

Ribbon lake formation

If you need to revise this subject more thoroughly, see the relevant topics in the *Letts* GCSE *Geography Study Guide*.

3 Weathering and glaciation

QUESTIONS

1 (a) Study the photograph below and the OS map extract (found on page 51) which show a glaciated area in the Lake District.

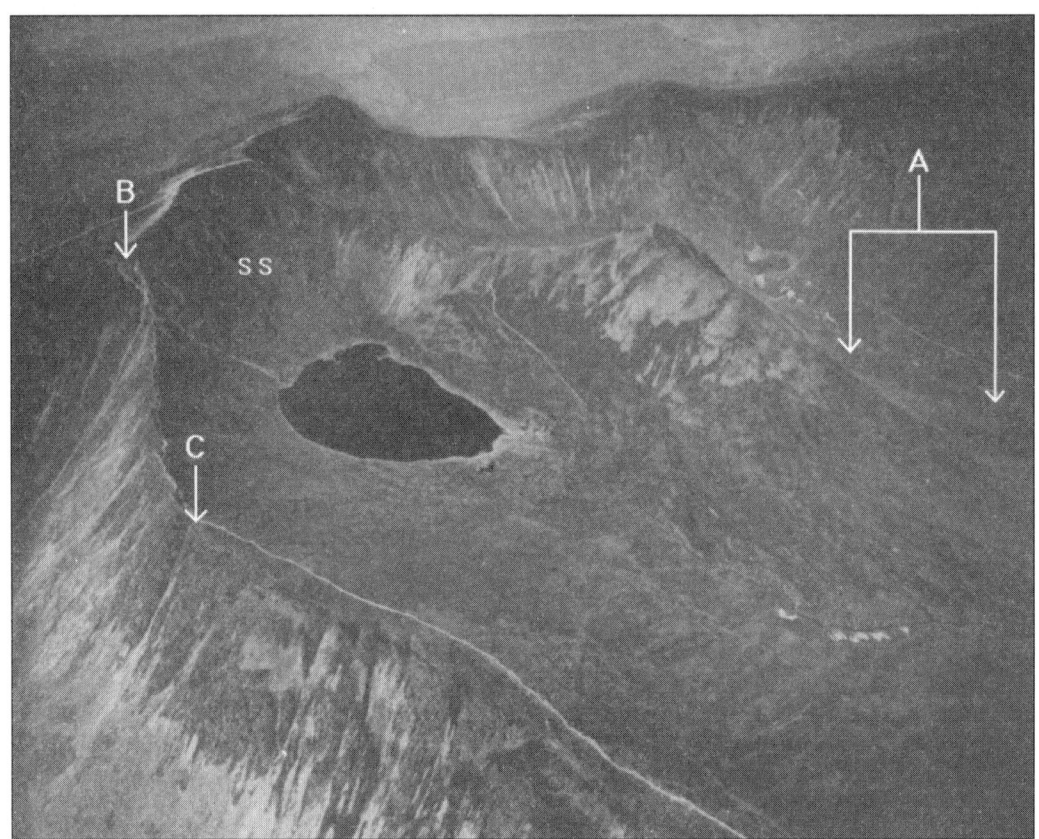

    (i) Name the landforms lettered A, B and C from the following list:

        Striding Edge   Glenridding   Helvellyn (3)

    (ii) Which of these is an arête? (1)

    (iii) Name the lake in the background of the photograph. (1)

(b) The steep slope marked **SS** on the photograph is an end product of weathering and erosion. On page 15 is a sketch of such a slope showing some weathering processes taking place.

    (i) Name the three types of weathering shown by the lettered arrows. (3)

    (ii) Which of these was most important during glacial times? (1)

    (iii) 1. What typical feature would you see on a landscape experiencing this type of weathering?

        2. Add this feature to the diagram. (2)

Weathering and glaciation 3

QUESTIONS

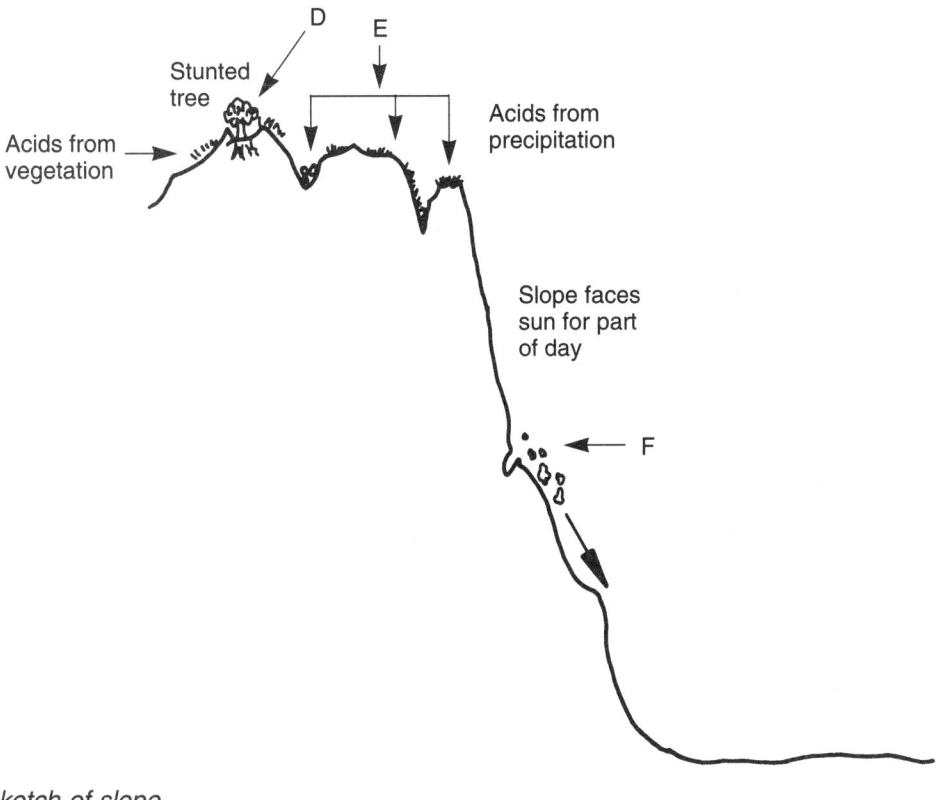

Sketch of slope

(c) The whole of the area in the south-eastern half of grid square 3415, surrounding Red Tarn, is called a corrie.

   (i) Using OS map and photographic evidence, describe its characteristic features. (3)

   (ii) Using labelled diagrams, explain how it was formed. (6)

(d) Some of the footpaths of this area stand out clearly as white lines on the photograph because of erosion.

   (i) Explain fully, giving at least three reasons, why footpath erosion begun by hill walkers, then worsened by a range of geomorphic processes, is often severe in regions like this. (6)

   (ii) What can be done to try and reduce the rate of soil erosion on such slopes? (4)

4 Weather and climate

REVISION SUMMARY

Weather relates to everyday changes in the atmosphere over an area; the climate is the averaging out of weather over a number of years.

Rainfall, high or low **temperature**, **fog**, **wind** and **sunshine amounts** are called **weather elements**. Factors which affect these elements and make them what they are, are termed **weather** or **climatic factors**. These include **latitude**, **altitude**, **seasons**, whether one is close to or far from the sea (**continentality**) and **ocean currents**.

- **Latitude** is important because the higher the latitude, the lower the angle of the Sun in the sky. The lower the angle, the less warmth the Sun gives.

- **Seasons** – In addition, because of the tilt of the Earth in relation to the Sun, higher latitudes have much more variation in the height of the Sun in the sky during the year and much more variation in the length of day and night than places in the tropics. So in northern Scandinavia (65 °N) days are long and the Sun fairly high in the sky during summer making it tolerably warm. In winter, the Sun is low in the sky, the days are very short (2 or 3 hours) and it is very cold. Near the Equator, the length of night and day and the height of the Sun vary little, so the weather and climate are similar throughout the year.

- **Continentality** – The sea, e.g. the North Atlantic, takes longer to warm up and cool down than the land surface, e.g. Europe, so it acts as a reservoir of heat in winter and coolness in summer. If winds blow from the Atlantic on to western Europe, i.e. are **onshore**, then this warmth or coolness is brought on to the land.

These controls and others are shown more clearly on the diagram below.

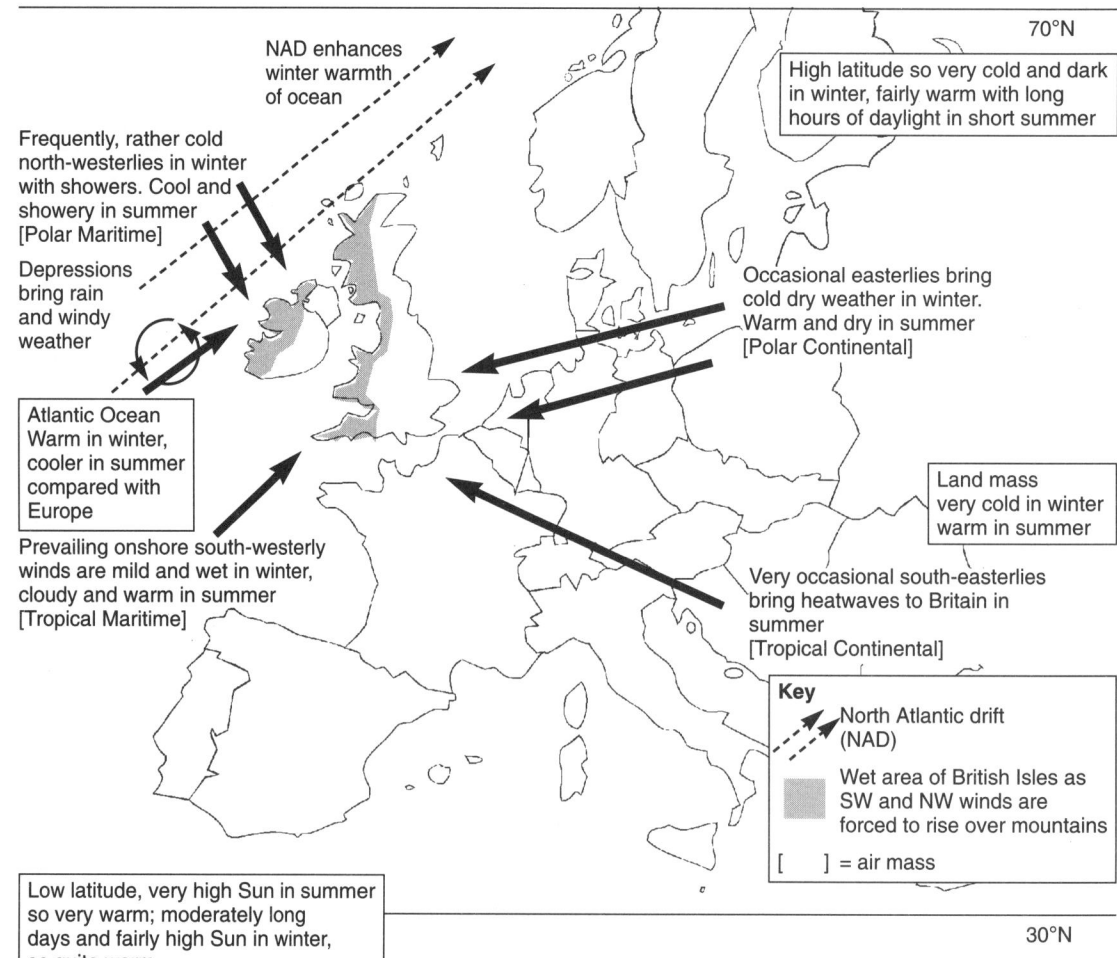

Factors affecting weather and climate of British Isles and adjacent parts of Europe

Weather and climate 4

Rainfall, or more correctly precipitation as this includes snow and hail, is the result of air rising, cooling, condensation taking place to form clouds, with precipitation often ensuing. Rainfall is usually classified into three types: **convectional**, **relief** (orographic) and **frontal** (cyclonic). This classification is based on the cause of the air rising. Convectional rain results from air rising because of the Sun heating the ground and warming the air above; relief rain results from air being forced to rise over high ground; frontal rain results from warmer air being forced to rise by colder air in a frontal depression.

REVISION SUMMARY

Characteristics of depressions and anticyclones

Air pressure is measured on a barometer and is usually expressed in millibars (mb). In our latitudes, low pressure is termed a **depression**, high pressure is called an **anticyclone**.

Depression	Anticyclone
Air moves anticlockwise, converges and rises.	Air moves clockwise, diverges and subsides.
Conflict of air masses causes further rising of air and precipitation at cold, warm and occluded fronts.	Homogeneous air mass and air stable. No fronts.
Weather: cloudy, windy, rain or showers. Mild in winter. Cool in summer.	Weather: little cloud, light winds, dry, night fogs. Cold in winter (frosts), warm in summer.
Air quality good, as pollutants are dispersed.	Air quality often poor. If a temperature inversion exists pollutants are trapped near the ground, giving smog in winter. Ozone in summer in cities caused by bright sunshine on car fumes.

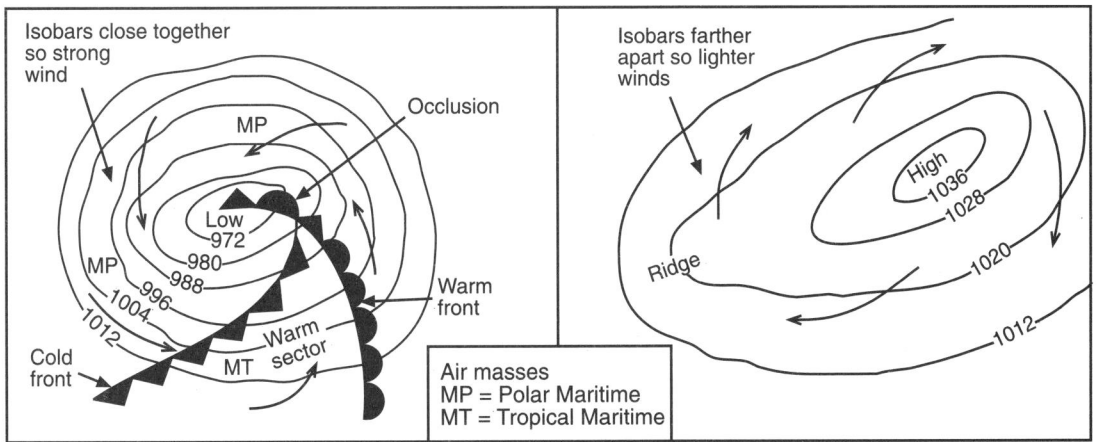

Weather elements, when combined together and averaged out over a period of 20–30 years, constitute the climate of a place. No two places have precisely the same climate, but places with similar climates can be grouped together. All places within a particular climatic region normally also share similar natural vegetation and soils. This is because these three components of the environment are interrelated.

17

4 Weather and climate

REVISION SUMMARY

Summaries of interrelationships in three climatic regions

Name and location	Equatorial: Amazon Basin, Congo Basin, Indonesia	Monsoon: South-east Asia	Cool Temperate Continental: Prairies and Steppes
Climate	Hot (27 °C) and wet (1500–2000 mm) all year round.	Tropical Monsoon. Hot/wet and cooler/dry season. Sometimes very wet (1000–2000 mm).	Long, cold winters with a little snow. Warm, showery summers.
Vegetation	Rainforests. Great variety of hardwoods. Forest appears green all year.	Monsoon forests. Jungle, almost impenetrable on hills, cleared on lowlands.	Short grassland of steppe and prairie types.
Soils	Red, deep, rather infertile – latosols.	On hills, tropical soils ravaged by erosion. In valleys, alluvial soils.	Fertile black earths (chernozems) or browner prairie soils.
Native way of life	Shifting subsistence agriculture. Crops – manioc, yams, hunting and fishing.	Intensive subsistence rice farming in valleys. Double cropping of rice. In cooler areas, rice and wheat. Terraced hillsides prevent soil loss.	Nomadic herding or hunting, e.g. Red Indians and bison.
Recent modifications	Forests felled for timber, mining and farming. Plantations set up.	Green revolution – hybrid strains. Intermediate technology, tea plantations.	Extensive grain farming – wheat, barley, some maize.

If you need to revise this subject more thoroughly, see the relevant topics in the *Letts GCSE Geography Study Guide.*

The British Isles experience a Cool Temperate Western Margin type climate. Although the climate of, for example, the Isle of Wight is not exactly the same as the Southern Uplands of Scotland, or for that matter South West France, there are sufficient similarities for all three to be classified as in the Cool Temperate type. Winters are mild and wet, summers are not too warm and still fairly wet. The whole of this region has a natural vegetation of deciduous forest – most of it cleared for farming – and possesses quite deep, fairly fertile brown forest soils.

Weather and climate 4

QUESTIONS

1 (a) Study the information about the Equatorial Rain Forests on Fig. 1.

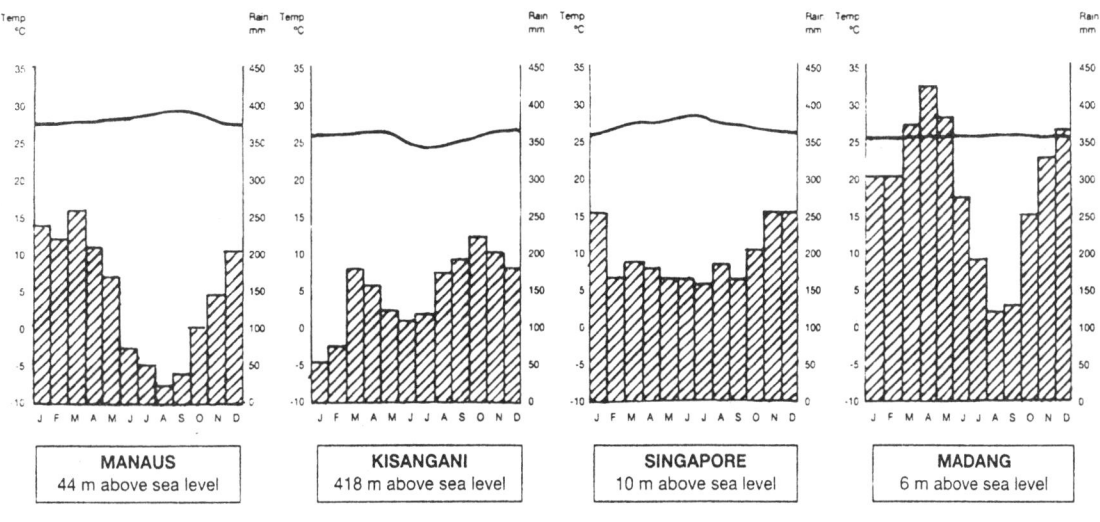

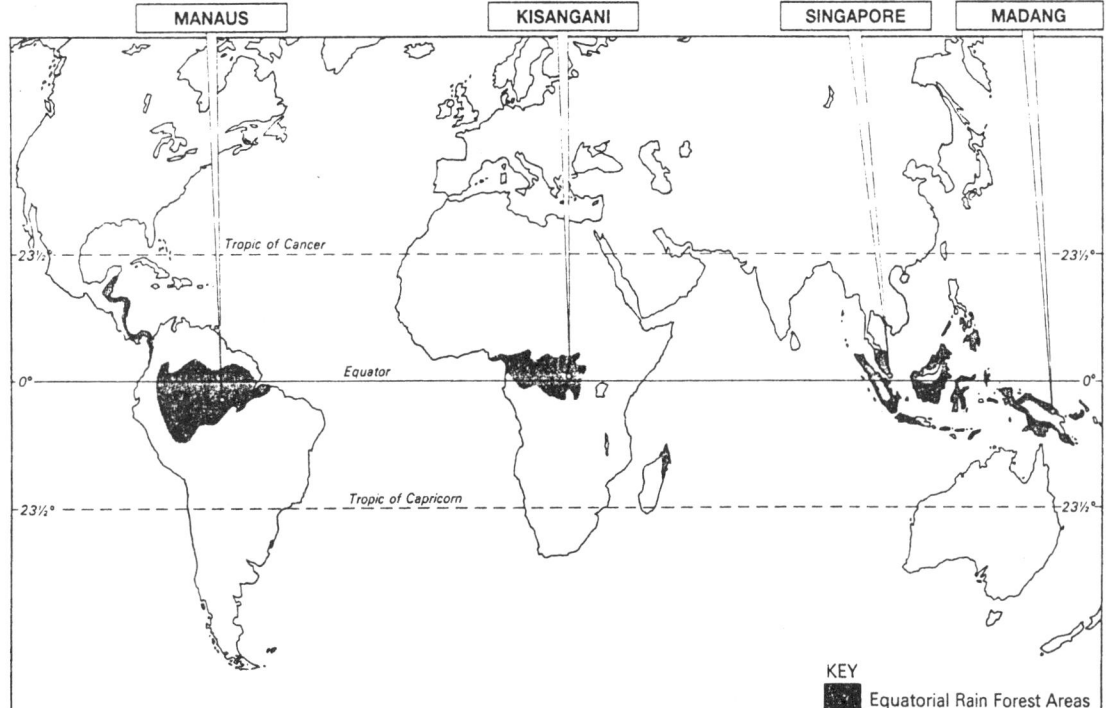

Fig.1

    (i) Describe the distribution of the Equatorial Rain Forest areas. (3)

    (ii) What is the average rainfall in Madang in January? (1)

    (iii) Why do Equatorial Rain Forests have a high annual rainfall? (3)

    (iv) What is the meaning of the term 'annual range of temperature'? (2)

    (v) State briefly why the annual range of temperature in Equatorial Rain Forest areas is so small. (2)

4 Weather and climate

QUESTIONS

(b) Study the weather map, Fig. 2.

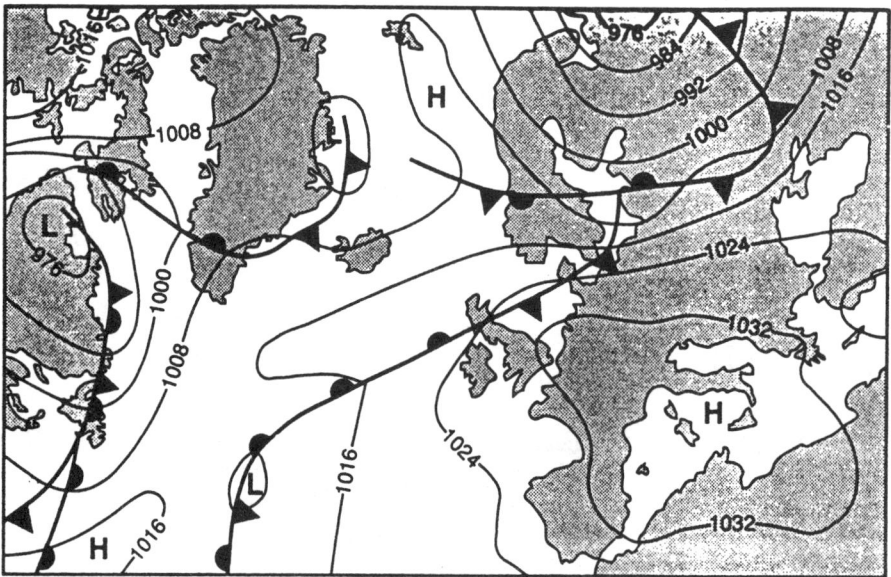

Fig. 2   © The Guardian 14.12.91

    (i) What units are used to measure atmospheric pressure? (1)

    (ii) What type of pressure system is shown over most of western Europe? (1)

    (iii) Winds over southern England on 14 December were light and southerly.

        (A) How does Fig. 2 suggest that the winds were light? (1)

        (B) Explain why the winds were southerly. (3)

(c) Study Fig. 3, a report on the very poor air quality conditions which existed in much of England at the time of the weather map shown in Fig. 2.

Phew! What a wheezer

Motorists in London were urged to stop driving by the Government yesterday as air pollution reached the highest levels since records began in 1976.

It was the first time the Department of Environment has called for voluntary restraint in using cars, which are the main cause of the 'very poor' air quality recorded at every one of the department's monitoring stations in the capital.

Asthmatics and people with chest complaints were urged by the Department of Health to stay indoors as much as possible and to seek medical advice if they begin to suffer from coughing, wheezing or shortness of breath.

Joggers and others taking exercise outdoors were advised to stop until the current cold, still weather ends.

People should avoid using streets with heavy traffic but that did not mean it was unsafe to go to work, or necessary to wear a mask.

A spokeswoman for the department appealed to the public to use public transport whenever possible.

There are four categories of air quality: very good, good, poor and very poor. Very poor is recorded when nitrogen dioxide reaches 300 parts per billion. Yesterday 382 parts per billion were recorded in central London, 388 in west London and 423 in south-west London.

In some parts of Europe, such as Holland and Denmark, local authorities can stop traffic and restrict industrial emission if air quality standards drop as far as those in London.

Fig. 3

Weather and climate 4

QUESTIONS

    (i) Use Fig. 3 to name:

        (A) the gas used as a measure of air quality. (1)

        (B) one health problem caused by the very poor air quality. (1)

    (ii) Suggest how the weather conditions shown in Fig. 2 would help cause the air quality found over much of the United Kingdom. (2)

    (iii) Why should governments encourage motorists not to use their cars in such weather conditions? (4)

SEG 1993

2 (a) Study Fig. 4, the satellite image and Figs. 5 and 6, synoptic charts.

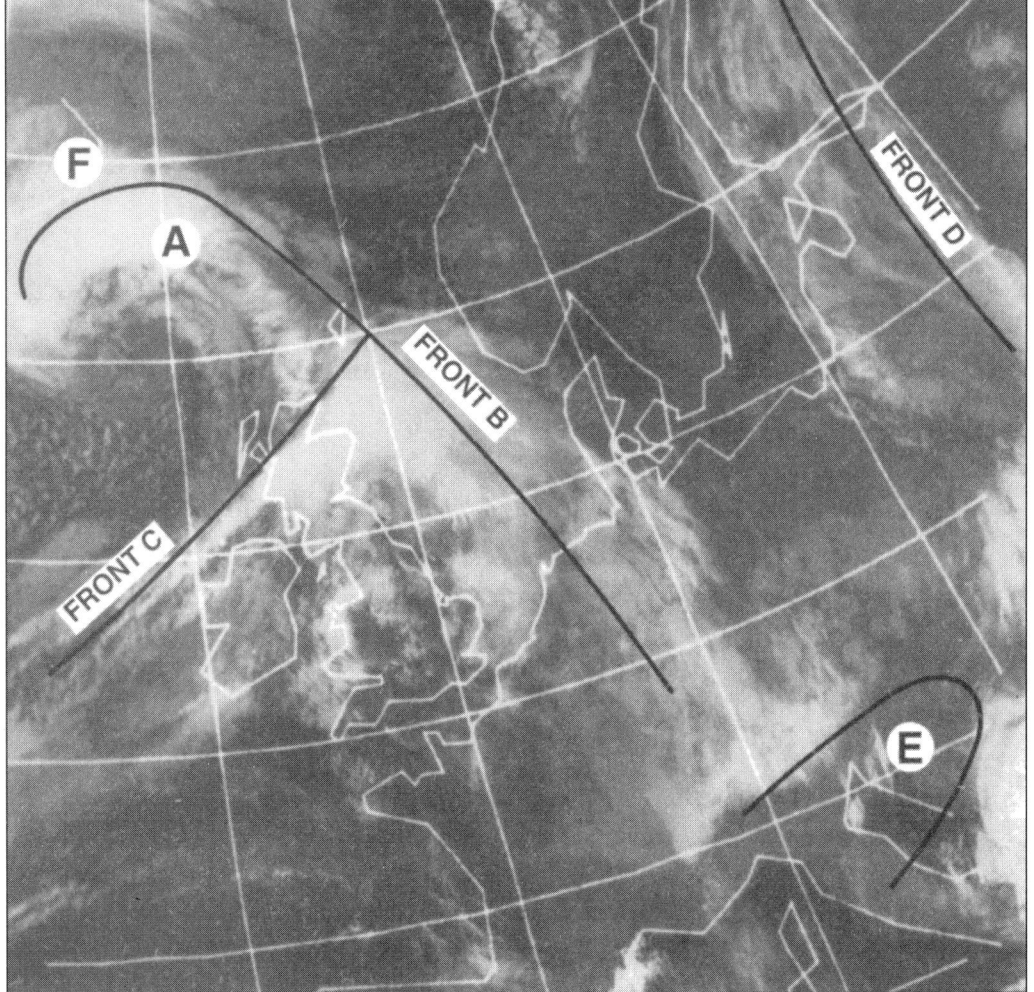

(Reproduced with kind permission from Dundee University)

Fig. 4 Satellite image – 3 a.m. 19 December 1991

4 Weather and climate

QUESTIONS

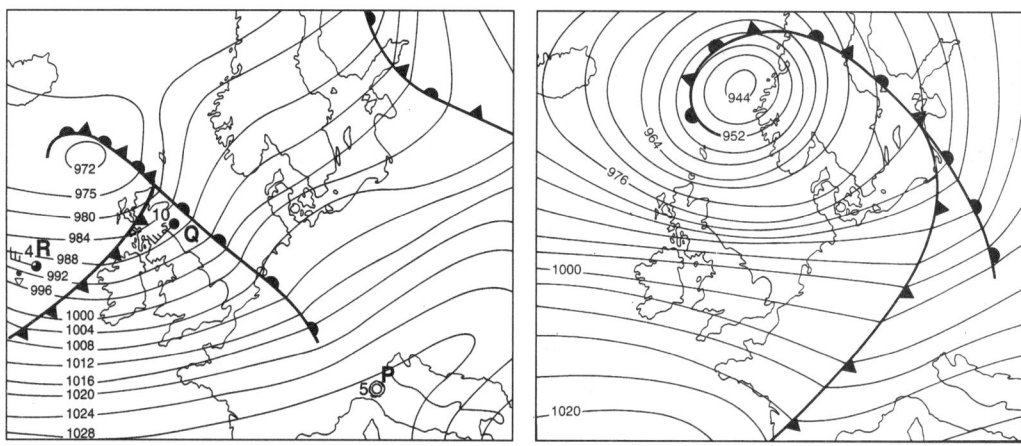

Fig. 5 Weather map – 3 a.m.
19 December 1991

Fig. 6 Weather map – 3 a.m.
20 December 1991

The satellite image has several features labelled. Using Fig. 5 to help you, identify

(i) weather system A, B, C, D, pressure feature E. (5)

(ii) Suggest **two** pieces of evidence that the line marking front B on Fig. 4 is located more than 100 km farther east than it should be. (2)

(iii) Explain why the cloud belt is curved at F. (2)

Study Fig. 5 only.

(iv) Describe the weather at Weather Station R. (3)

(v) In what way can the **satellite image** help support your description of the weather at Weather Station R? (2)

(b) Using Fig. 5, explain the temperature conditions at Weather Stations P, Q and R.

(i) Weather Station P

(ii) Weather Station Q

(iii) Weather Station R (6)

(c) Refer to Fig. 6, a weather map showing the situation 24 hours later.

(i) Describe how weather system A and its fronts changed over the 24 hours. Give **four** changes. (4)

(ii) Write a weather report to describe and explain **two** features of the weather for Britain at 3 a.m. 20 December 1991 (Fig. 6). (6)

WJEC 1993

Population and resources 5

REVISION SUMMARY

Distribution of population

At present there are over 5 billion people living on Earth. The world's population, however, is not spread evenly across the globe. In fact, half the world's people occupy only one twentieth of the land surface. Human beings can only live where conditions are right for life, so people are attracted to the most suitable areas. Few people live where a hostile environment or the lack of essential resources would make life difficult to sustain.

Most people live where conditions are favourable, for example:

- where farmland is fertile and suitable for growing crops
- where the climate is pleasant and equable
- where important minerals such as coal are found
- where flat land allows towns and cities to be built.

Few people live where conditions are unfavourable, for example:

- high latitudes where temperatures are too cold
- hot deserts which are too dry
- jungles which are too dense to penetrate
- mountains which are too steep to build on.

The number of people per unit area is called the **population density**. In some parts of the world the population density is high. For example, parts of Hong Kong have over 6000 people living in every square kilometre. Actual figures for population density can be misleading.

It is not the total number of people that is important but whether or not an area has sufficient resources to support the number of people who want to live there.

If an area cannot support its population then that area is said to be **overpopulated**. For example, the Netherlands has a population density of 970 people per square kilometre but is not overpopulated because it is a wealthy country which has developed its resources to a point where it is able to support its population. Ethiopia has a population density of 45 people per square kilometre but, in parts, is considered overpopulated because a rapidly growing population, a series of droughts and agricultural mismanagement have used up the country's resources of land and food at a rate too great to be sustained.

Population pyramids

The shapes of **population pyramids** can tell you quite a lot about the countries they represent. A triangular shape, like that shown in Fig. 1 below, will tell you that this country is part of the economically developing world, where birth rates are high (hence the broad base) and expectation of life is fairly low (hence the rapidly narrowing top). If the pyramid is more pillar shaped, like that shown in Fig. 2 below, it signifies that this country is in the economically developed world. Here the birth rate is much lower – almost as low as the death rate – so this country's population is virtually static, as long as there is no significant gain or loss from migration.

If you need to revise this subject more thoroughly, see the relevant topics in the Letts GCSE Geography Study Guide.

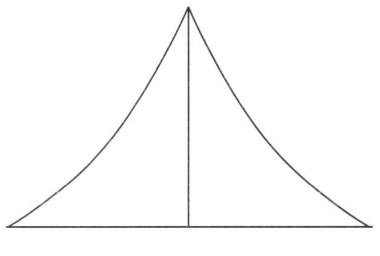

Fig. 1

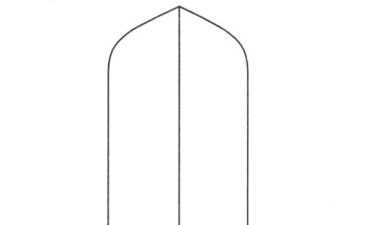

Fig. 2

5 Population and resources

QUESTIONS

1 (a) Study the age/sex pyramids shown in Fig. 3.

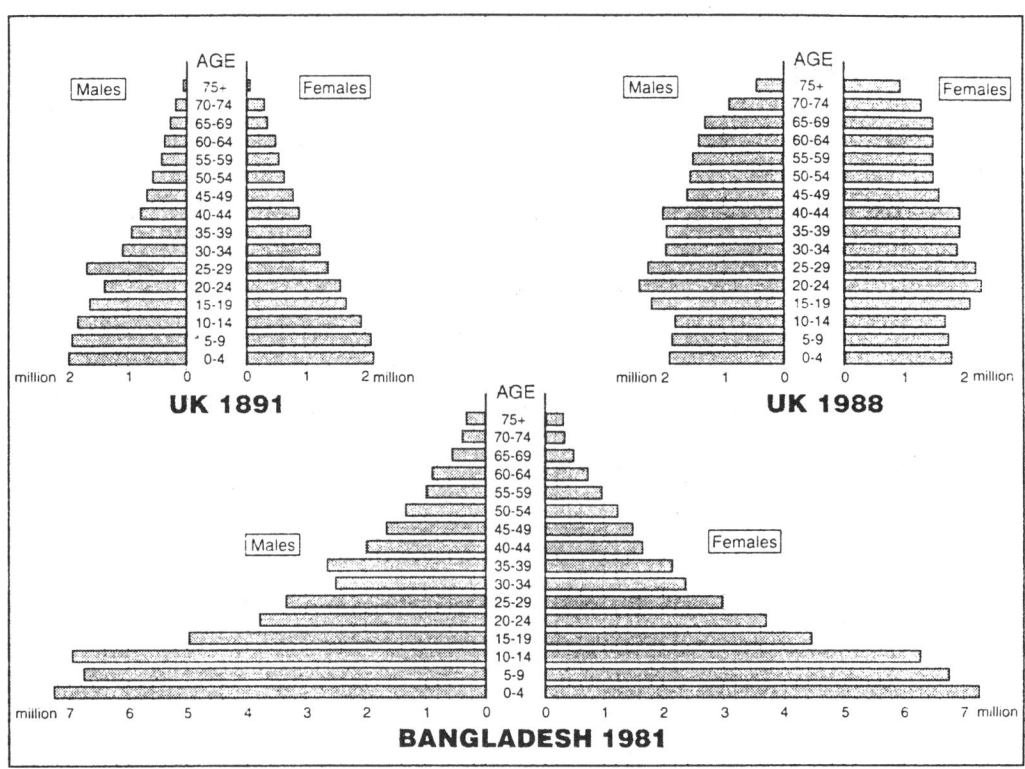

Fig. 3

    (i) What is a census? (1)

    (ii) In what ways is the shape of the pyramid for the UK in 1891 similar to that for Bangladesh in 1981? (2)

    (iii) Describe the changes that have taken place to the United Kingdom's age/sex pyramid between 1891 and 1988. (3)

    (iv) Explain the issues which result from the changes in the UK's population structure. (4)

    (v) Why do some people disagree with controlling population growth? (3)

(b) Study Fig. 4 on page 25, showing the population density of different countries.

    (i) What is the meaning of the term population density? (1)

    (ii) Which of the countries named on Fig. 4 has the highest population density? (1)

    (iii) Why can information on population density be more useful than figures which show only a country's total population? (2)

    (iv) 'Physical factors cause variations in population density throughout the world.' Comment on this statement, with reference to places you have studied. (8)

Population and resources 5

QUESTIONS

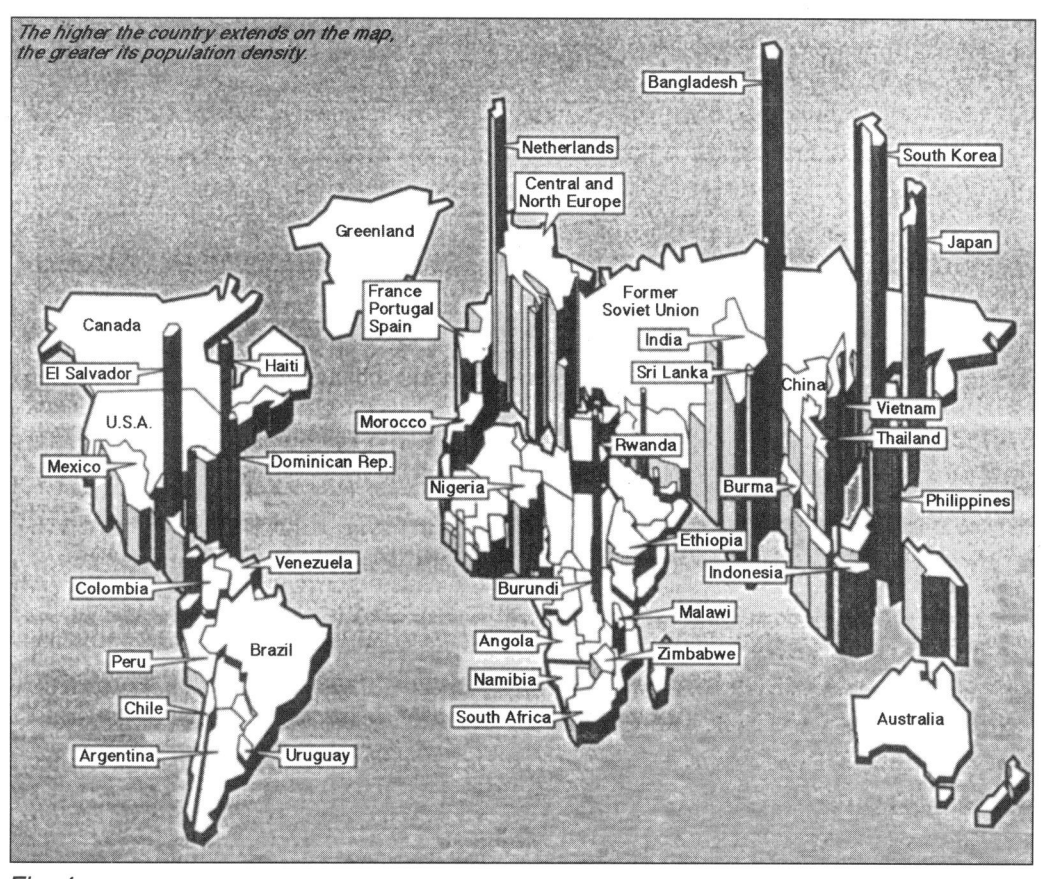

Fig. 4

SEG 1993

6 The Urban World

REVISION SUMMARY

Soon most of the World's population will be living in urban areas. Towns and cities have distinct patterns of land use. Urban land use is usually studied using a model. Models are used in geography a lot. A model represents a perfect situation and is used to simplify reality. Real life situations can be very complex and difficult to understand but comparing them to a model allows us to see how they differ from the norm.

The Concentric Ring Model (after Burgess) and the Sector Model (after Hoyt) are two common models used in geography. Land use in a typical British city is a combination of the two models as shown below.

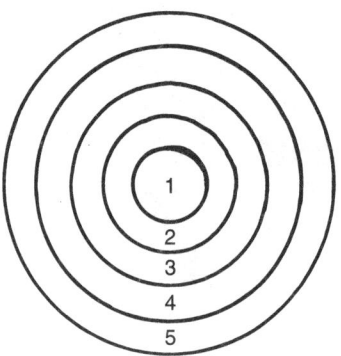 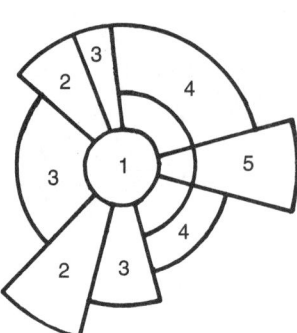 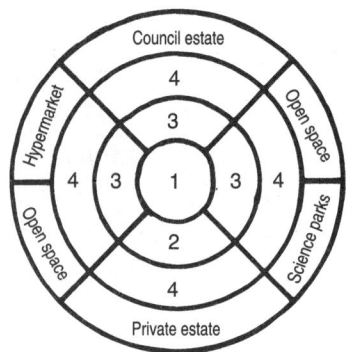

Key: 1 = CBD, 2 = Transitional zone, 3 = Low class housing, 4 = Medium class housing, 5 = High class housing

The Concentric Ring Model   *The Sector Model*   *A typical British city*

CBD (Central Business District) – this is where land is at its most expensive. A modern city centre contains high rise office blocks, covered shopping arcades and pedestrianised streets. No houses are found here and there is very little open space.

Inner City – around the CBD is an area that was built in the last century. It is usually an area of industrial decline with high density terraced housing built to house factory workers. Many factories and old housing have been demolished and the land redeveloped.

Inner suburbs – a residential area with many houses built during the 1920s and 1930s.

Outer suburbs – the newest part of the town with mixed land use. Included here would be new housing estates, council estates, out-of-town shopping areas, modern industrial parks and open space.

Greenbelt – an area around the city boundary where planning controls limit development.

There are many problems associated with living in the modern city:

- high crime rates
- high levels of unemployment
- poor air quality and other forms of pollution
- traffic congestion
- poor housing quality and urban decay
- areas of ethnic segregation which sometimes lead to violence and unrest.

As a result of these problems many people are moving out of the inner city into the surrounding countryside. People are moving out to rural areas so the population of many cities is falling. This is called counterurbanisation.

Retailing – a changing urban land use

Retailing is the selling of goods to the customer. A **consumer** is someone who buys goods from a shop. **Low order, convenience** goods, such as bread, milk and newspapers, are bought on a daily basis. Usually people would not be prepared to travel far in order to purchase such items. **Middle order, comparison** goods, such as shoes and clothes, are bought less frequently.

The Urban World 6

Consumers compare prices and styles before deciding which items to buy. **High order, luxury** goods, such as jewellery and furniture, are only bought occasionally. Usually people are prepared to make a special journey and to travel further in order to purchase high order goods.

The **range** of an item or service is the maximum distance people would be prepared to travel in order to purchase that item or to obtain that particular service. The lower the order, the shorter the range. The **threshold** of an item or service is the minimum number of customers needed in order to make a profit. The higher the order, the greater the threshold.

Shops can be placed in a hierarchy depending on the types of goods they sell. Each shop should be sited at a location that best suits the type of goods they sell. A good location could lead to many customers and a healthy profit. A poor location could mean a business would struggle to survive.

Types of shop

Corner shops – these are located within walking distance of people's homes. They sell low order, convenience goods and are open for long hours, e.g. 7 a.m. to 10 p.m. for example. They cater for people who work late or for those who have forgotten or run out of something. The corner shop is often the hub of the community with many customers known personally to the shop owner.

Shopping parade – here 5–15 shops are found in the suburbs, usually along main roads. They sell a mixture of comparison goods and convenience goods. There may be several **specialist shops**, such as a bakery, a chemist and maybe a Post Office.

Large department store – found in the centre of the town. It offers a wide range of high order goods in different departments, such as TVs and videos in the electrical department, furniture and maybe even carpets. People are prepared to make a special journey in order to visit the shop.

Superstore – a modern development. A large shop, over 2500 m^2, found on the outskirts of the town. Superstores, such as Sainsbury and Tesco, have been attracted to edge-of-city locations as:

- they are near main roads, giving easy access for both customers and delivery lorries
- land is cheaper
- there is plenty of space to build a large store plus room for car parking and for lorries to turn
- the congestion of the town is avoided.

Superstores attract customers by:

- staying open late
- selling products at a cheaper price than smaller shops (they can do this because they sell goods in bulk)
- offering free car parking and cheaper petrol
- providing a coffee shop and/or cafeteria.

Recent trends in shopping

Shopping is a major growth activity in Britain today. In the past shops were always located in the town centre. People moved from shop to shop, along crowded pavements as traffic rolled past on the main road. Very little thought was given to the needs of the shopper and shopping was considered to be a necessary evil. Today many town centres have been pedestrianised with trees, benches and fountains. Town centres have been forced to make these changes in direct response to the growth of out-of-town shopping areas. There is competition for customers and people will shop where the shopping is made more attractive. Superstores, hypermarkets and even large shopping malls are now found on the edge of many towns. Shopping habits have changed for the following reasons:

- refrigeration and domestic freezers mean food can be kept fresh for longer
- more people work and do not have the time to shop as frequently
- the number and range of pre-prepared 'ready meals' has increased
- people are prepared to travel further to shop as car ownership has increased
- being paid monthly means that people find it more convenient to buy in bulk
- increased affluence has created a demand for more luxury items.

REVISION SUMMARY

If you need to revise this subject more thoroughly, see the relevant topics in the *Letts* GCSE *Geography Study Guide*.

6 The Urban World

QUESTIONS

1. (a) Study Fig. 1

   (i) Label each of the following land uses in the spaces marked 1, 2, 3 and 4 on Fig.1.

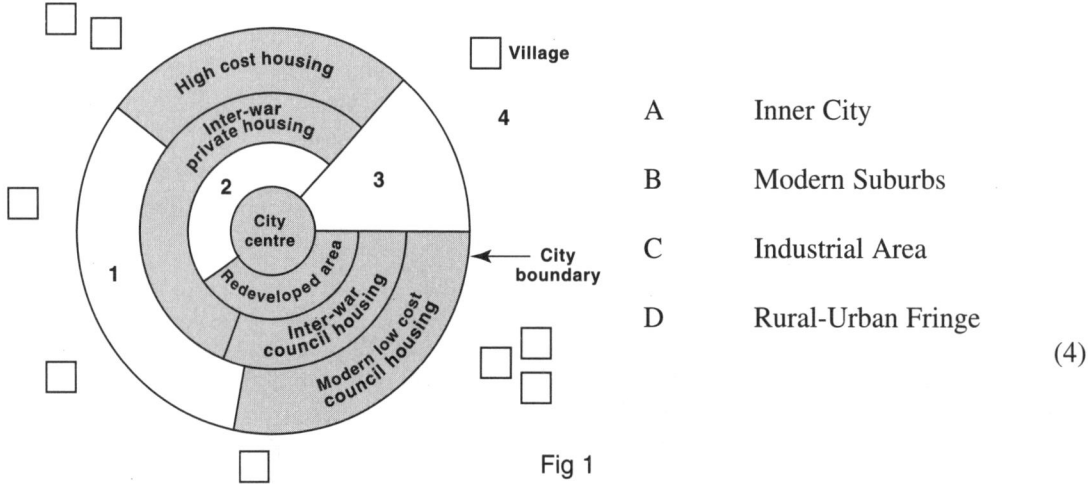

   A   Inner City

   B   Modern Suburbs

   C   Industrial Area

   D   Rural-Urban Fringe

   (4)

   Fig 1

   (ii) Describe three features of the city centre (6)

   (iii) Which area of a city do you think would have traffic congestion? (1)

   (iv) How are people trying to solve the problem of traffic congestion in a city or town you have studied? (5)

   (b) Study Fig. 2.

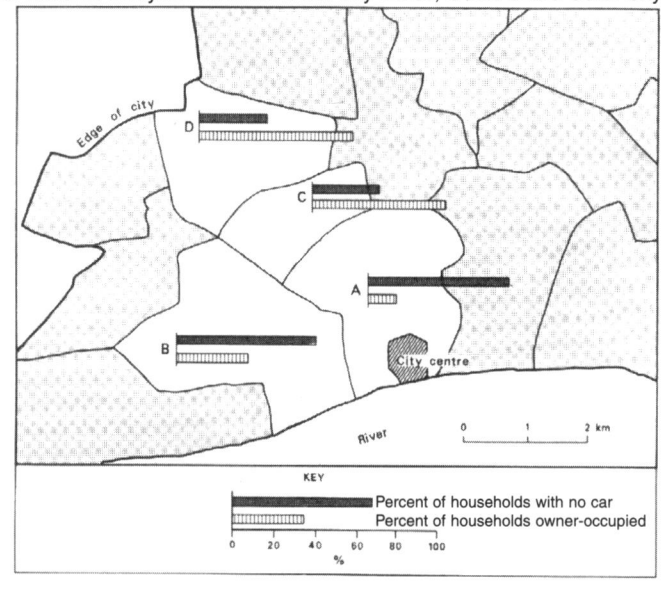

   Figure 2 Four wards of a city. A and B are Inner City wards, C and D are Outer City wards.

   (i) Study the two statements below.

   Statement P: *"The percentage of owner occupied housing is greatest near the edge of the city."*

   Statement Q: *"The percentage of owner occupied housing varies very little in a city."*

The Urban World 6

State which one seems to be more accurate. Justify your choice
using evidence from Fig. 2 (4)

(ii) Suggest two reasons for the difference in car ownership between
wards A and D. (4)

(c) A survey of shopping habits in and around a city produced the results shown in Figs. 3a, b and c.

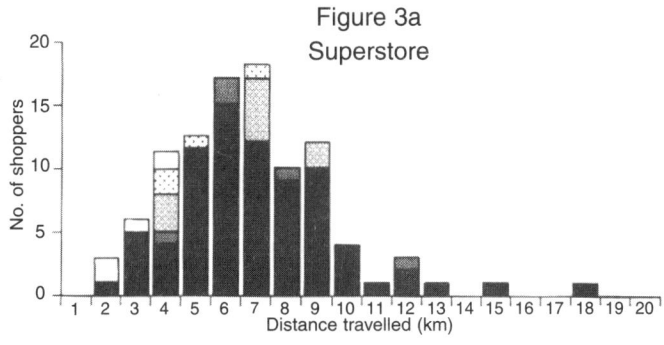

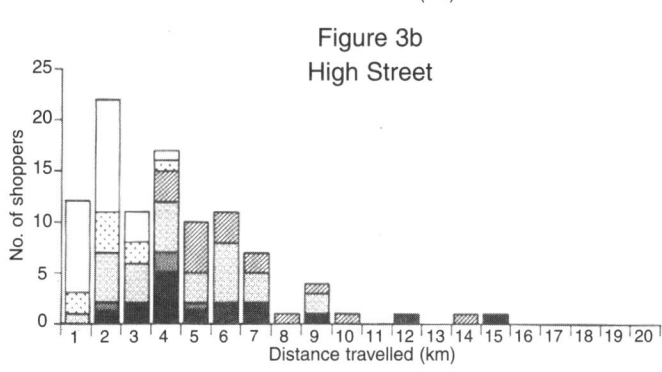

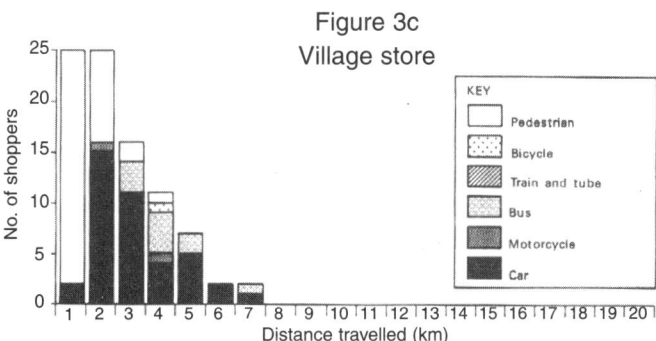

(i) What do Figs. 3a, b and c tell you about the shopping habits of people using Superstores and people using the High Street? (6)

(ii) With the help of Fig. 3c, describe and explain the shopping habits of people using small shops such as a village store. (6)

(iii) What is the effect on each of the following of building large out-of-town shopping developments?

City Centres

The areas in which Superstores are built (6)

MEG 1996

7 Urbanisation

REVISION SUMMARY

In 1850 there were two cities in the world with a population of over one million. In 1990 there were nearly 300.

This statement highlights two remarkable trends in world population during the last one hundred and fifty years 1. the accelerating increase in world population numbers and 2. the ever increasing proportion of it living in towns and cities. This second trend is called **urbanisation**.

Urbanisation started in a significant way some two hundred years ago in the countries of North West Europe where the Industrial Revolution was first experienced. The early mining and manufacturing industries drew people to work in them from the rural areas, where life was hard and poor. Around these industries towns were built, some of which merged into conurbations at a later date. Now more than 75% of the population in More Economically Developed Countries (MEDCs) live in urban areas. More recently urbanisation has become a world-wide phenomenon, for the percentage of the total population living in towns in Less Economically Developed Countries (LEDCs) has been increasing rapidly. (See Fig. 1).

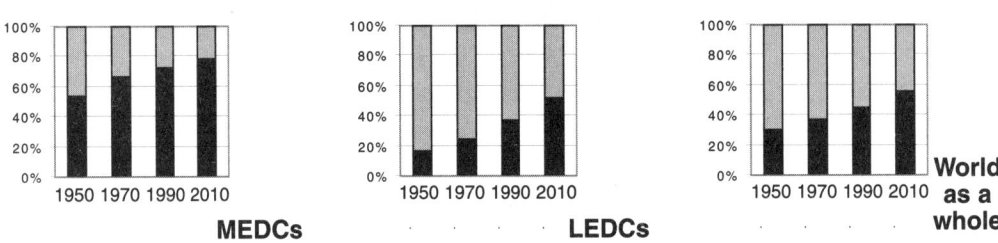

Figure 1:
Growth in urban populations: global trends and projections

Proportions of population living in urban centres (%)
Source: United Nations

The increasing urbanisation of the LEDCs is demonstrated by Figs. 2 and 3 below. In 1950 seven of the ten largest cities in the world were in MEDCs; in 1995 there were only two – New York and Tokyo. Soon, more than half of the total world population will be living in urban areas.

There are two important differences to note between urbanisation in the nineteenth century and early twentieth century in MEDCs and twentieth century urbanisation in LEDCs. In the MEDCs people moved into the towns to satisfy the towns' ever increasing demand for labour. Population numbers in many rural areas fell. Death rates in the cities were almost as high as death rates in rural areas, so the major reason for the increase in urban numbers was immigration from the

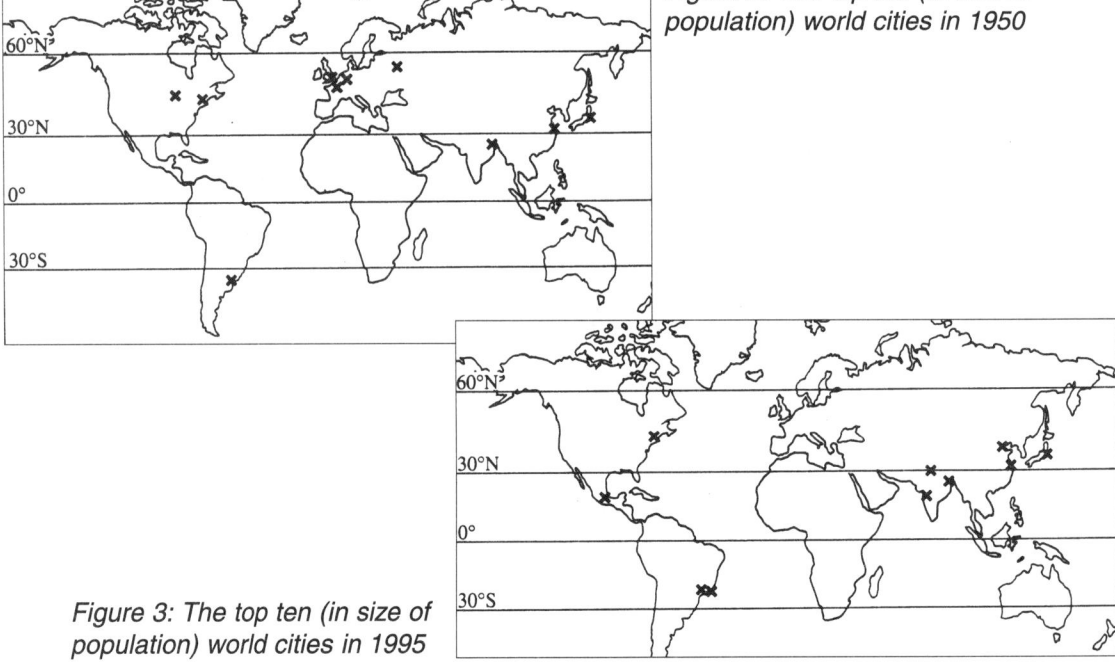

Figure 2: The top ten (in size of population) world cities in 1950

Figure 3: The top ten (in size of population) world cities in 1995

Urbanisation 7

REVISION SUMMARY

countryside. In twentieth century urbanisation in LEDCs migrants move into the cities in hope of a job. Except for the shanty towns, death rates are lower than in rural areas. Birth rates, though falling slowly, remain high. Thus the rapid growth in urban population numbers is as much due to natural increase within the urban areas as it is to migration.

Two sets of factors are recognised as bringing about rural to urban migration in LEDCs. They are **push factors** and **pull factors**.

Push factors are those that **force people out** of rural areas. They include:

- changes in farming methods, e.g. mechanisation, which mean fewer people are needed to work farms.
- Floods, droughts and other disasters which, besides physical damage, cause crop failure and lead to famine.
- The division of farms by inheritance laws so that plots of land become too small to support a family.

Pull factors are those that **draw** people into urban areas. They include:

- opportunity for work, hence a pay packet and higher living standards.
- A better welfare infrastructure of, e.g. schools, health facilities, leisure opportunities.
- A chance, in the longer term at least, of better housing.
- The belief that self advancement will be easier in a city than it is in the rigid social structure of rural areas.
- A chance to enjoy the 'bright lights' that the media have made people aware of.

Many of these pull factors have proved illusory. Most cities receiving these migrants suffer from many severe **problems**.

- The population is growing so fast that there are not enough jobs to meet demand.
- There is just not enough accommodation at the right price.
- Roads are often choked with traffic leading to heavy pollution.
- Public services such as water supplies, sewerage, schools and hospitals are overstretched.
- There is a lack of public transport which prevents the poor migrant from travelling to find or attend work.

Thus many migrants end up settling into a shanty town, maybe with some of their village friends, at the edge of the city. These shanty towns (other names for them are bustees or favelas) are beset with most of the problems listed above as well as others. The houses are usually built of cardboard, plastic or metal obtained from rubbish heaps. There is overcrowding and disease is rife. People live on the margin of survival. They live there because they have nowhere else to go. Eventually, with luck, they will get a job and things will improve. Usually these jobs are of an **informal** kind. That is, the worker is self employed, the job is labour intensive, materials used are cheap, and there are no fixed work hours. Such jobs range from shoe cleaning to street trading to general repair work.

Sometimes, city authorities and shanty town dwellers come together and develop self-help schemes to improve matters. The dwellers build and maintain simple brick and mortar houses with the authorities providing basic services. In a few cases in LEDCs, new towns have been built to relieve the overcrowding. One of the best-known schemes is at Cairo.

In a few MEDCs, such as the UK, urbanisation appears to have peaked. Many people, given the opportunity, would choose to live in rural rather than urban surroundings. Easier commuting, the growth of modern industries on the edges of towns and developments in telecommunications, which allow people to work from home, have allowed such workers to exercise this option. Thus some town populations have fallen and the population of the surrounding rural area has risen. This fairly recent population trend is called **counterurbanisation.**

If you need to revise this subject more thoroughly, see the relevant topics in the *Letts* GCSE *Geography Study Guide.*

7 Urbanisation

QUESTIONS

1 (a) Study Fig. 1 below, a graph showing urban growth in India 1951-91.

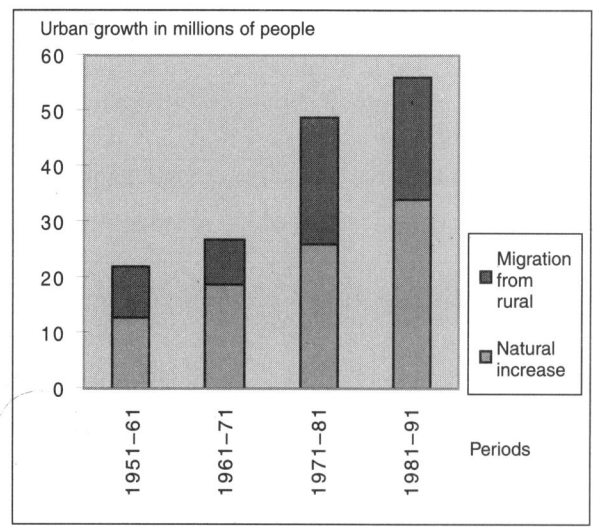

Figure 1: Urban growth in India 1951–1991

(i) What was the size of India's urban growth in the period 1951–61? _____ millions

(ii) What was the **main** cause of urban growth in India between 1951 and 1991?

(iii) In which ten year period did migration from rural areas have the greatest effect on urban growth in India? (3)

(b) Study Fig. 2 below, a map showing the place of origin of migrants to Bombay in India.

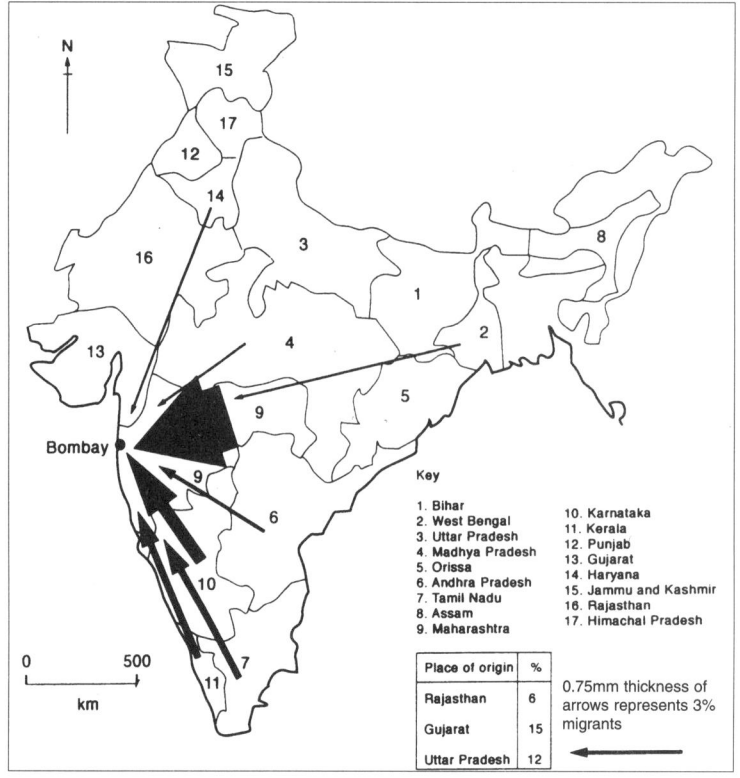

Figure 2: The place of origin of migrants to Bombay

Complete the map of India, using information from the table in the key. (4)

Urbanisation 7

(c) (i) Using your finished map (Fig. 2), complete the following sentence

"Generally the number of migrants gets smaller as the distance of their place of origin from Bombay gets _____ "

(ii) Suggest **TWO** reasons for the pattern described in your answer to (c) (i)

(iii) Using Fig. 2 name the Indian state which is the main exception to the pattern described in (c) (i)

(iv) Suggest **TWO** reasons which could explain why that state is an exception. (6)

(d) Study Fig. 3 below, a map showing a development plan for Bombay in 2001.

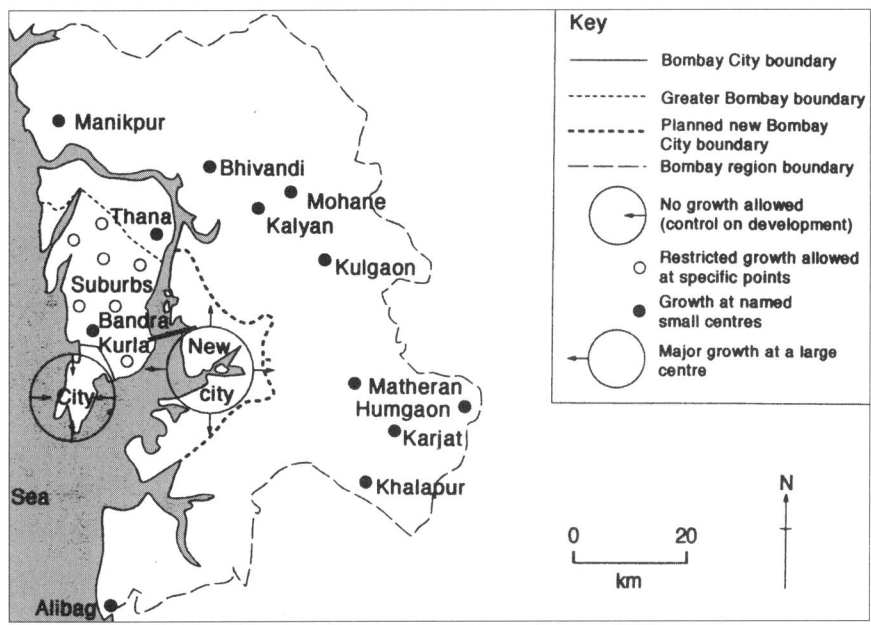

Figure 3: A development plan for Bombay in 2001

(i) On what physical feature are the present city and suburbs built?

(ii) Using Fig. 3 describe fully how the development plan aims to deal with future population growth in the Bombay area. (4)

(e) **Name** a town or city outside the United Kingdom (apart from Bombay) that has recently experienced rapid urban growth.

(i) Describe the problems that have resulted there from urban growth.

(ii) Explain how the town/city planners are trying to deal with those problems. (8)

LONDON 1995

8 Agriculture

REVISION SUMMARY

Farming is classed as a **primary** industry. It extracts produce in a renewable way from the Earth's surface, either directly through crops or indirectly via livestock. Many farm products can only be grown economically in certain parts of the world, and so farm produce plays an important role in world trade, often earning LEDCs (less economically developed countries) valuable foreign currency. For example, many Caribbean countries earn significantly from their exports of crops, such as bananas and sugar, to North America and Europe. Farming can be classified under many different headings:

- **Subsistence** – where farmers produce for their families, with little to spare
- **Commercial** – where farmers try to make a profit by selling their produce
- **Arable** – where farmers concentrate on growing crops, such as cereals or vegetables
- **Pastoral** – where farmers are concerned with livestock, such as sheep and cattle
- **Mixed** – where farmers combine both pastoral and arable farming
- **Intensive** – where the farm has a high output per unit of land but not necessarily per unit of labour, e.g. subsistence rice growing or market gardening
- **Extensive** – where the farm has a high output per unit of labour but a lower output per unit of land, e.g. cereal farms on the Prairies
- **Plantations** – where multinational companies grow one or maybe two crops on a large estate, usually in tropical LEDCs, for export to MEDCs (more economically developed countries).

Combinations of farming types

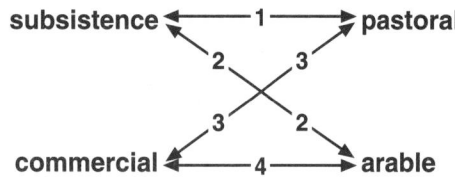

Examples of combinations

1	N. Scandinavia	Lapps and Reindeer	E
2	River valleys of India	Rice growing	I
3	Hills of N.W. Europe	Sheep farming	E
3	Lowlands of N.W. Europe	Dairying	I
4	Prairies of N. America	Cereal cultivation	E
4	Near major towns	Market gardening	I
4	Tropical regions	Plantation farming	I

E = extensive   I = intensive

If you need to revise this subject more thoroughly, see the relevant topics in the Letts GCSE Geography Study Guide.

Farm systems

All farms are run as a system with inputs, processes and outputs. The **inputs** determine the nature of the farming. In the past, **physical geography** (such as relief, soil and climate) exerted a very powerful influence. This is still the case in most LEDCs. But **economic**, **political**, **scientific** and **technological** factors have become more significant in most MEDCs. These factors include the size and closeness of the market; the quality of the communication system; government policies on production limits, pricing and subsidies; scientific developments in curing crop and animal diseases; and the development of new high-yielding, disease-resistant varieties of crops (such as the new rice varieties which have contributed to the **green revolution** in India and Pakistan).

Impact on the environment

In some parts of the world, rainfall is low and irregular, notably in the Sahel in North Africa. What had been sensible cropping and grazing during the wet years, became **overcropping** and **overgrazing** during the dry years. This led to the destruction of the natural vegetation and soil structure, and to the soil's eventual erosion by water and wind to create a barren region. This is called **desertification**.

Agriculture 8

QUESTIONS

1 (a) Study Fig. 1 below, a graph showing the average monthly rainfall and temperature at Cape Town, South Africa.

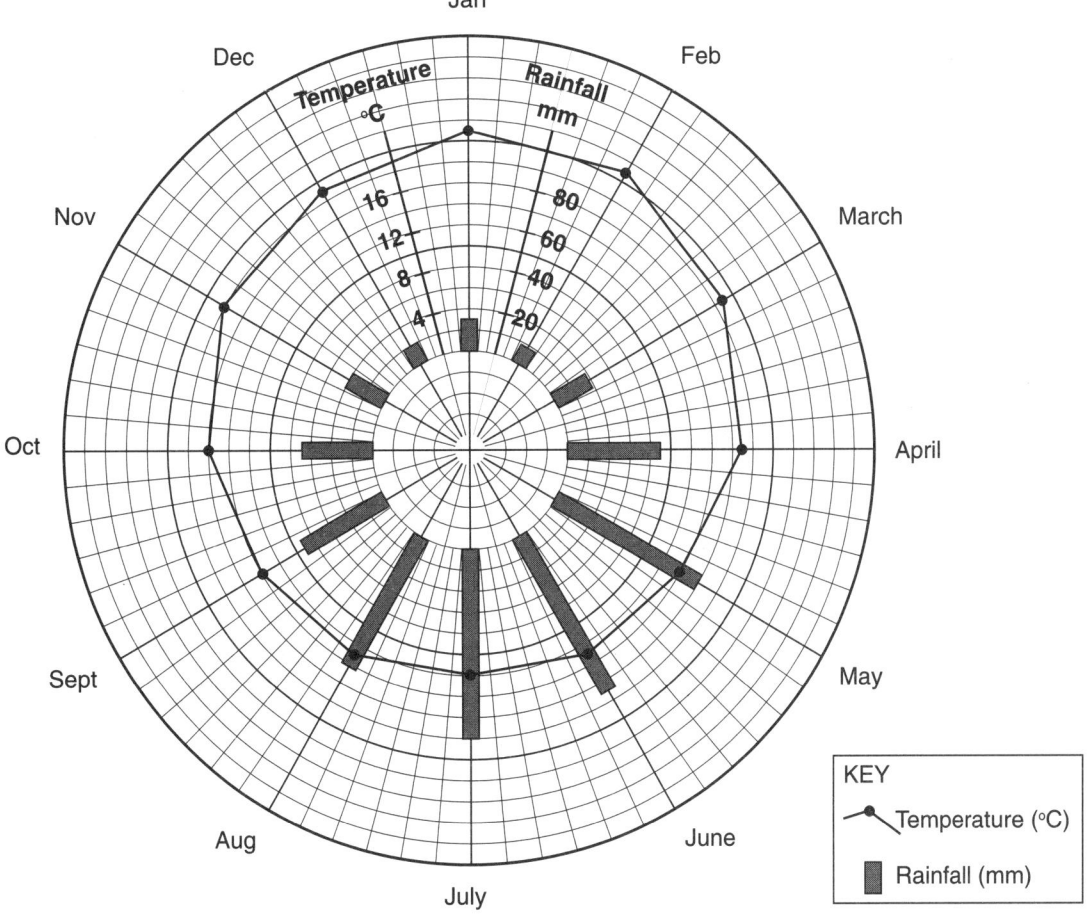

Fig. 1 Average monthly rainfall and temperature at Cape Town, South Africa (Latitude 33° 54′S, Longitude 18° 32′E, Altitude 17 metres)

  (i) Name the coolest month and give its temperature.

  (ii) Name the **three** months when farmers will probably **most** need to irrigate (water) their crops.

  (iii) Give **two** reasons for your answer to (a) (ii).

  (iv) Are the three months you have named in (a) (ii) in winter or summer? (5)

 (b) Study Fig. 2 on page 36, a cross-section through Lourensford Plantation, a fruit farm 50 km east of Cape Town.

  (i) State the compass direction which the slope in Fig. 2 faces.

  (ii) Complete the following sentence:

   The orchards range in altitude from .... metres to .... metres above sea level.

  (iii) The temperatures shown in Fig. 1 are rather high for growing apples and pears. Using Fig. 2, explain fully why temperatures will be lower at Lourensford Plantation. (5)

8 Agriculture

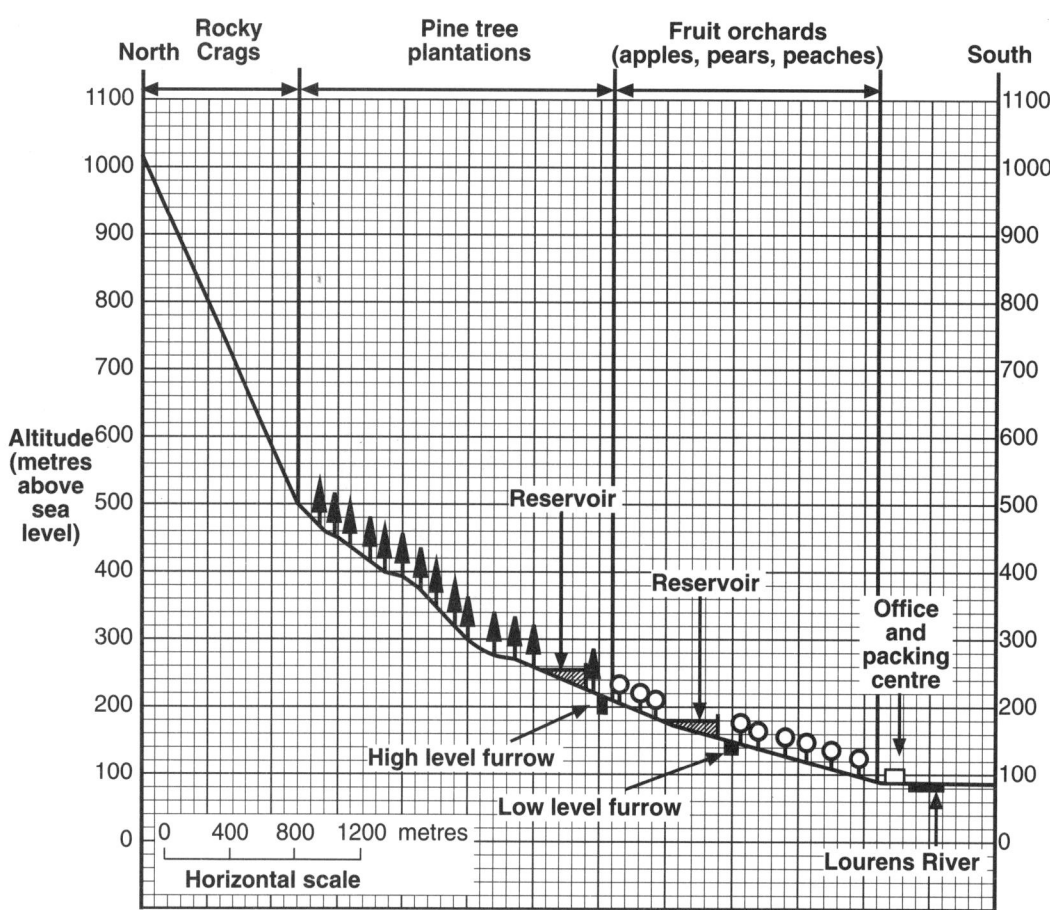

Fig. 2 Cross-section through a fruit farm near Cape Town, South Africa

> The first orchards were planted immediately above the office and packing centre. They were watered by the Low Level Furrow, which came from a small reservoir on the slope above. As the farm expanded, greater water supplies were needed. A high level dam and the High Level Furrow were then built to serve the new orchards.
>
> The furrows (open, cement-lined channels) follow the contours. Irrigation in the orchards is by overhead sprinklers, which are fed by underground pipes from the furrows.

Fig. 3 Irrigation on the fruit farm

(c) Study Fig. 2 again, and then Fig. 3 which gives information about irrigation on the farm.

  (i) State the **two** devices used to take water from the reservoirs to the sprinklers in the orchards.

  (ii) The Lourens River flows through the farm. Using information from Fig. 2 suggest in full why the irrigation water was **not** taken from this river.

  (iii) Suggest **three** reasons why the farmer planted pine trees on the upper slopes of the farm. (6)

(d) For a farm that you have studied in a **named developed** country:

  (i) Draw a systems diagram showing the farm's inputs, processes and outputs.

  (ii) Explain why the farmer chooses to practise that type of farming. (9)

LONDON 1995

Manufacturing industry 9

REVISION SUMMARY

As explained in Unit 11, **manufacturing** makes up the **secondary** sector of industry. To manufacture means to make something in a works or factory. In industry, to manufacture means to make something in a factory. Each factory can be looked at using a systems approach. **Costs of production** and the **raw materials** that go into the factory would be the **inputs**, jobs done in the factory would be the **processes** and the **finished products**, which the factory sells, would be its **outputs**.

Industrial location

There are many things a company must consider before deciding where the best location for their business would be. Locational factors include:

- the site – is a large or small area of land needed and is it flat?
- raw materials – are they light or heavy and bulky? Do large amounts need to be imported?
- market – is it close, is it local or global?
- labour – is there an adequate supply? Is there skilled labour available?
- transport – are links to markets good?
- capital – is there enough money available?
- incentives – are grants, tax-free benefits or low rents available for certain areas?
- agglomeration – would it be an advantage to locate close to companies producing a similar product?
- inertia – perhaps it is more expensive to relocate than stay put.

There is no perfect location for a factory. After considering all the factors, the final decision will represent the best compromise location.

Industrial change

Changing energy: From the late eighteenth to the early twentieth century industry in the UK depended on coal for its power. Coal was bulky and expensive to transport, so industries such as iron and steel, shipbuilding, heavy engineering and chemicals as well as the textile industries, located themselves on or close to the coalfields. These industries employed many of the UK's increasing working population. Thus the coalfields and some coastal locations such as London and Belfast, to which coal could be imported cheaply by water, became the UK's major population centres.

Now manufacturing industries are largely powered by electricity, a form of energy which can be transported fairly cheaply via the National Grid to any location in the UK. Therefore most industries are now freer to chose their location. They respond to looser locational factors such as markets and routeway accessibility. In short, the majority of modern manufacturing industries are much more **footloose** than their predecessors.

Decline and growth: Coalfield regions, such as parts of Central Scotland, NE England and South Wales, once so important for their heavy industries, suffered a dramatic industrial decline during the two middle quarters of the twentieth century. It proved difficult to attract alternative industries to these regions because of their blighted industrial landscapes, poor communications and poor housing stock. The consequences of decline were:

- high unemployment, especially of males;
- run down of services as the population's spending power dwindled;
- out-migration to the Midlands and the South East of England.

These two regions attracted the migrants because:

- modern footloose industries were growing up;
- there were better communications and more modern housing;
- the landscape was undamaged so therefore more attractive;

9 Manufacturing industry

REVISION SUMMARY

- London, as the capital, acted as a magnet for all kinds of economic activity;
- in these regions, there was more and more work available in the tertiary sector (see Unit 11) which began to supersede the secondary sector as the major employer of labour.

Government intervention: To try and remedy matters in those regions where there was high unemployment and poverty, the governments of the day created 'Development Areas'. In these areas they tried to attract new industries by:

- improving the infrastructure by building new roads;
- offering financial aid in the form of grants, rent free periods, reduced interest rates and tax relief on equipment;
- improving the environment by reclaiming industrial wastelands;
- offering training schemes for the unemployed;
- setting up 'enterprise zones' and 'urban development corporations' specifically aimed at rejuvenating derelict city centres.

These measures have met with a fair degree of success. Excluding Northern Ireland, where there are special circumstances, unemployment levels have tended to even out throughout the UK. Many large firms have relocated in these 'development areas'. Besides British companies. American, Japanese and German firms have been prominent. These include, for example, Sony and Panasonic in the electrical field and Nissan, Honda and Bosch in the motor vehicle field. Many non-European firms have established themselves here to be within the tariff walls of the European Union.

Other Locational Trends: Freed from the locational constraints operating earlier this century, many footloose industries have located close to each other. This process of **agglomeration** occurs to take advantage of **economies of scale**. By collaborating with adjacent, similar firms, the individual firms may save money through bulk buying, in sharing improved communications, in sharing financial service. Again firms can 'feed off' each other – for example,. products, or even the waste of one factory may be used in another. This process of agglomeration is widespread, but is particularly prevalent at motorway intersections, e.g. M4 and M5 near Bristol, and close to urban by-passes as industry has shifted from the inner city to more accessible edge-of-city sites.

The success of an industry in an area may generate other forms of economic development. The increased prosperity of the workforce and possible increases in population in the area will increase demands for service industries of all kinds from health and education facilities to shopping and entertainment provision. The consequential development is referred to as the **multiplier effect**. For example, the proposed South Korean electronic factory development near Newport in South Wales will employ 6000 workers directly, but is expected to generate another 15000 jobs in the area through linked industries and the provision of services.

If you need to revise this subject more thoroughly, see the relevant topics in the Letts GCSE Geography Study Guide.

Manufacturing industry 9

QUESTIONS

1 (a) In the nineteenth century heavy industry developed in many areas in Britain, in other parts of Europe, and in North America. Examples of 'heavy industry' are:
iron and steel making, shipbuilding, railway engineering, chemical manufacture, armaments manufacture, textile manufacture.

    (i) Name a region where heavy industry developed. This can be in Britain, or any other part of the world.)   (1)

    (ii) Describe the industry, or industries, that developed there.   (3)

    (iii) Explain why the region was suitable for that industry, or industries.   (6)

(b) Many Japanese firms have recently built factories in areas where traditional heavy industry has declined. Study Figure 1 below.

Company	Products	Number of Workers
Sony	TV tubes	2400
Toyota	Car Engines	2300
Matsushita	TVs, microwave ovens	1475
Sharp	Video recorders, microwave ovens, typewriters, photocopiers	1300
Hitachi	TVs, video recorders, hi-fi equipment	864
Brother	Typewriters	700
Orion	Video recorders	680
Aiwa	Audio and compact discs	520

Figure 1 : Major Japanese companies with factories in South Wales

    (i) Describe the type of industry that has been set up by the Japanese in South Wales.   (3)

    (ii) In 1973 the United Kingdom joined the Economic European Community (European Union). Since then many Japanese firms have built factories in old heavy industry areas in the UK, such as South Wales. Suggest two reasons why Japanese firms built factories in areas like this.   (4)

(c) Industry in Less Economically Developed Countries (LEDCs) in the 'Poor South' is, usually very different from industry in the More Economically Developed Countries (MEDCs) in the 'Rich North'.

Describe what the industry is like in LEDCs using some, or all of the following headings. Refer to one or more areas you have studied.

Raw materials Labour Energy Markets Capital Technology Transport   (6)

NEAB 1996

10 Tourism and leisure

REVISION SUMMARY

Tourism is the industry that caters for people who want a holiday. Over 70% of people living in the UK took some kind of holiday in 1993, though for some it was just a day trip. Tourism is a major industry, providing 18 million jobs for people across Europe. Places people visit for a holiday are called resorts. The tourist industry has grown rapidly over the last thirty years. This is because:

- people have more leisure time owing to working shorter hours, having paid leave from their work or retiring at a younger age
- people have become wealthier, so they have more money to spend on luxuries such as holidays
- more information is available about other places so people want to visit them
- it is easier to get to places that were once considered far away
- a wide range of purpose-built resorts and package holidays has become available.

There are many different types of holiday, for example:

- **long stay summer resorts** These attract people who want to spend a week or more in one centre. They are usually found on the coast next to sandy beaches, e.g. in the countries around the Mediterranean Sea. Tourists are attracted by the warm, dry, sunny weather, excellent beaches and a warm sea to swim in, bars, night-clubs, discos and other beachside facilities, and a variety of good standard accommodation which caters for families with young children. Most of the resorts can also be reached easily, being only two to four hours flying time away. A **package holiday** is where one payment is made and the tour operator arranges the flight, accommodation, airport transfers, meals and entertainment.

  Despite the lure of the Mediterranean, most British holiday-makers take their summer holiday in Britain. The most popular destinations are the south coast and south-west of England where the weather is usually better. Many British holiday resorts now offer a wide range of facilities that cater for the whole family, especially attractions that do not depend on hot, sunny weather.

- **long haul** Such holidays are becoming more popular. This is where tourists travel long distances to far away, exotic places such as Australia and New Zealand, Africa, the Far East or the Caribbean. Many developing countries, such as Kenya and The Gambia, are trying to expand their tourist industry. They see it as a means of improving their economy.

- **short-stay attractions** These are usually visited by people on day trips or on short breaks. These places have to be easy to reach. Included here are towns which are known for their culture, history or art. In Britain, a popular destination for a short break or day trip is any one of the eleven **National Parks**. These are areas of 'outstanding natural beauty' which have been set aside for special protection. Each National Park Authority has to protect and enhance the landscape, carefully manage the economic activities that take place in the park – e.g. farming, forestry, quarrying – help the public to participate in recreational activities, and give care and consideration to those people who live and work in the park. Every year, nearly 100 million visitors enjoy the scenic attraction of these diverse landscapes.

- **winter holidays** Since the late 1970s, winter sports holidays have become very popular. Areas such as the Alps have seen a large increase in the number of visitors. This has led to a huge growth in the skiing industry and in the number of tour operators offering skiing holidays. A number of purpose-built ski resorts have sprung up in response to the growing demand. Skiing is a very specialised activity and requires specialist facilities. Ski runs (pistes) have to be prepared, ski lifts installed, hotels built, medical facilities made available and a range of evening entertainment activities offered.

The influx of many tourists to an area can, in many cases, result in a **conflict** of interests. For example:

- **coastal areas** Around many parts of the Mediterranean, the building of holiday resorts has created an unbroken urban landscape. This has led to the clearing of the natural vegetation, the

Tourism and leisure 10

destruction of many wildlife habitats and has forced local farmers to move inland. Local resources, such as water, are often stretched to the limit.

Even in Britain, coastal environments are sensitive. For example, where sand dunes exist constant trampling can lead to severe wind erosion, walkers damage coastal paths and more tourists mean more noise, more litter and more pollution.

- **National Parks** Conflicts may arise over how best to use the land. There are many interested parties. For example, farmers may want to use more land at the expense of the Forestry Commission; the Ministry of Defence owns large tracts of land that they use for military exercises; water companies may want to build more reservoirs; industry may want to extract natural resources such as rock in quarries; property developers may want to build new homes. There may even be conflict of interest between different groups of people who use the park for leisure: water sports enthusiasts will disturb fishermen, horse riding may conflict with ramblers.

- **winter sports** Mountain environments, such as the Alps, are very fragile. Large numbers of tourists attracted to the mountains to ski can seriously affect the delicately balanced ecosystem. Types of damage include:
  - bulldozing slopes for ski runs compacts the soil, reducing infiltration which leads to an increase in surface run-off. As a result, there is an increased risk of flooding and soil erosion is more likely. The threat of flooding is greater during spring when snow melt swells rivers **and** during summer when thunderstorms bring heavy rain.
  - providing tarmac areas for car parking has the same effect as above
  - removing trees increases the risk of avalanche
  - skiing down a mountain on a thin snow cover can damage delicate plants underneath.

REVISION SUMMARY

If you need to revise this subject more thoroughly, see the relevant topics in the *Letts* GCSE Geography Study Guide.

10 Tourism and leisure

QUESTIONS

1 (a) A family received these four postcards from their friends who had gone on holiday.

> **A** The weather is wonderful; not a cloud in the sky and the temperature is about 28 °C every day. The beach is lovely and sandy and there is a really great night life in the clubs and discos. Of course we have tasted the local wine!
>
> **B** It is very cold here, but we have had lots of sunshine. The snow is deep and crisp. We went walking on a glacier yesterday, and I saw a corrie and an arête, just like those we studied in Geography.
>
> **C** We have tried out lots of activities like abseiling, pot-holing and walking. The weather is cloudy and cool. The scenery is so wild and beautiful, with outcrops of grey-white rock. It is quite clear why this area became a National Park.
>
> **D** Our hotel is very modern. Temperatures are very high every day, so we are glad of the beautiful swimming pool. The scenery is spectacular but the people live in great poverty in the shanty towns and subsistence farming villages away from the resort area.

(i) Five holiday resorts are marked on the map below, with boxes. **Four** of these places are described in the postcards.

Show which place is described in each of the postcards **by writing each letter, A, B, C and D, in its correct box on the map.** (4)

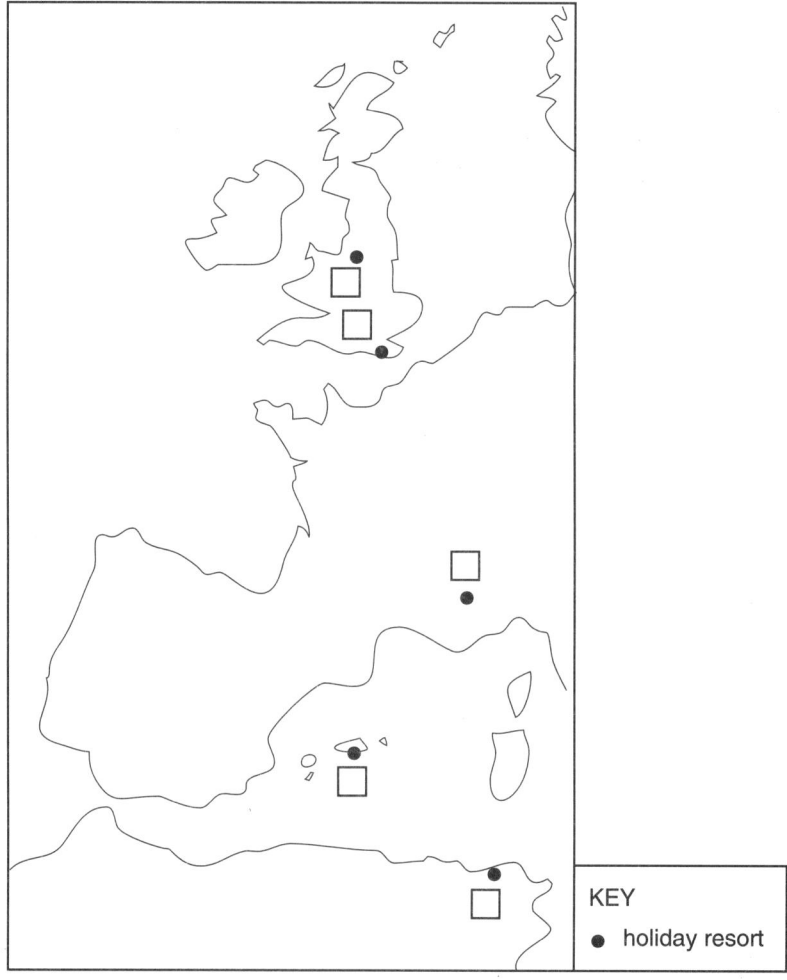

42

Tourism and leisure

(ii) Write a brief description of **either** a corrie **or** an arête. (2)

(iii) Postcard C was written from an area with some limestone scenery. How can you tell? (2)

(iv) Postcard C was written from a National Park. Give **one** of the main reasons why National Parks were set up in England and Wales. (2)

(v) Tourists can sometimes come into conflict with other land users in the National Parks. Describe **two** ways that conflict can happen. (2)

(vi) A tourist industry can bring both advantages and disadvantages. Describe **some of** these advantages and disadvantages. Use places and examples you have studied. (6)

(b) Study the climate graph for a holiday resort in the French Alps.

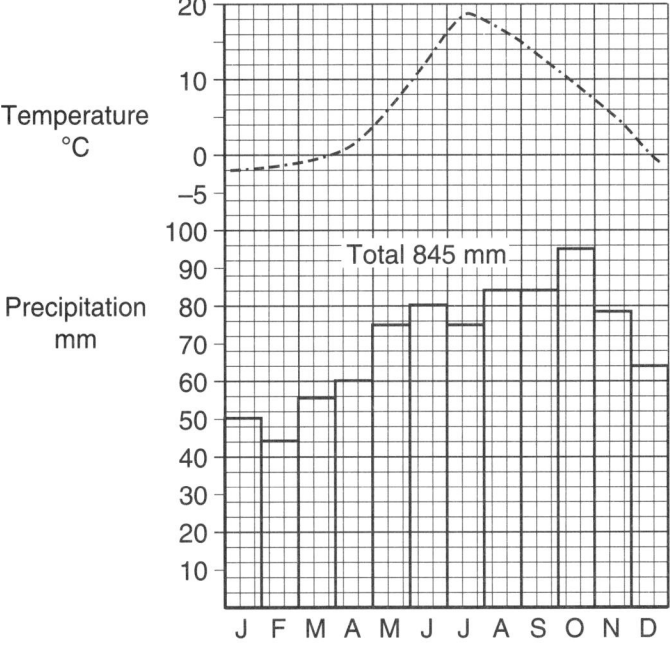

The climate of this area makes it popular for holiday makers from the United Kingdom. Explain why, using evidence from the graph. (3)

(c) Look at the photograph and the diagram on page 44. They show an Alpine resort.

(i) Describe both the natural tourist attractions **and** the man-made tourist attractions of the area shown above. (6)

(ii) Some people say that developing the ski industry in the Alps has damaged the environment. Suggest why. (3)

10 Tourism and leisure

QUESTIONS

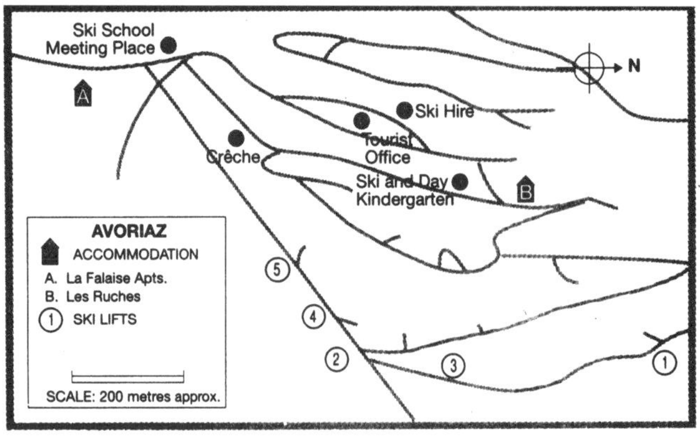

*Photo/map by permission of:
Thomson Tour Operations 1992*

NEAB 1993

Employment structures in developed and developing countries (MEDCs and LEDCs) 11

REVISION SUMMARY

Industry can be classified into four sectors – primary, secondary, tertiary and quaternary.

- Industries in the **primary** sector extract minerals, crops and fish from the Earth's surface.
- Industries in the **secondary** sector use and/or process some of the products of primary industry and from them manufacture goods that people need. For example, iron ore once it has been mined (primary) is converted into iron and steel (secondary processing), then into a whole range of products such as wire, girders, car bodies (secondary manufacturing).
- **Tertiary** industries provide back-up services. They include office work, retailing, entertainment, transport and financial services. Most of these are found in urban areas.
- **Quaternary** industries include the new hi-tech information services such as computer software. This is the industrial sector that has developed most recently.

  The relative importance of each of these individual sectors changes as a country develops.

- A country at an early stage of industrial development is dominated by primary industry (farming and possibly mining). Such countries often export the primary products to the economically developed world. They may become dependent on one or two products, e.g. Nigeria on oil, Sudan on cotton, and be at the mercy of fluctuations in commodity prices.
- The next stage of development shows growth of employment in the secondary industrial sector, i.e. in manufacturing, and a decline in employment in the primary sector as primary industries become more mechanised or mineral resources begin to run out. Usually, among the first manufacturing industries to develop are the textile, footwear and food processing industries. They are reasonably labour intensive so take advantage of low wage rates, have a large internal market, have locally available raw materials and do not demand too much sophisticated equipment.
- As a country reaches a more advanced stage of development, the primary sector shrinks to a low level. The secondary sector also declines, but less so. The tertiary sector expands rapidly as service industries (administration, commercial, welfare, medical, tourist) develop.

Characteristics of developing and developed countries

LEDCs (less economically developed countries)	MEDCs (more economically developed countries)
High birth rate, falling death rate, so rapid population growth	Low birth rate, low death rate, usually population growth is slow
Nutrition often below level for good health	Generally good nutritional levels
Low doctor/nurse: population ratio	Many more doctors, nurses and hospitals
Literacy rates quite low	Literacy rates at a high level
Poorly developed communication networks	Dense road and rail networks
Lack investment capital so money borrowed from World Bank and countries in the developed world – some have massive debts	Money and know-how often invested in developing countries – many loans are still outstanding
Primary industries dominate, so low GNP (gross national product)	Secondary and tertiary sectors dominate, creating considerable wealth, so high GNP
If at stage of manufacturing industrial growth, many people move from rural to urban areas, one result is shanty towns	In more advanced countries, major cities decline in population as people move to rural areas and commute to work
Most are in Africa, Asia and South America	Most are in Europe and North America

11 Employment structures in developed and developing countries

REVISION SUMMARY

Triangular graphs and scatter graphs

The **triangular graph** is often used to show employment structure. At first glance it is not that easy to read. Study the example given below carefully. In this case:

A – Tanzania = 80% primary, 6% secondary, 14% tertiary
B – Italy = 14% primary, 43% secondary, 43% tertiary

Work out the readings for C, which is the UK.

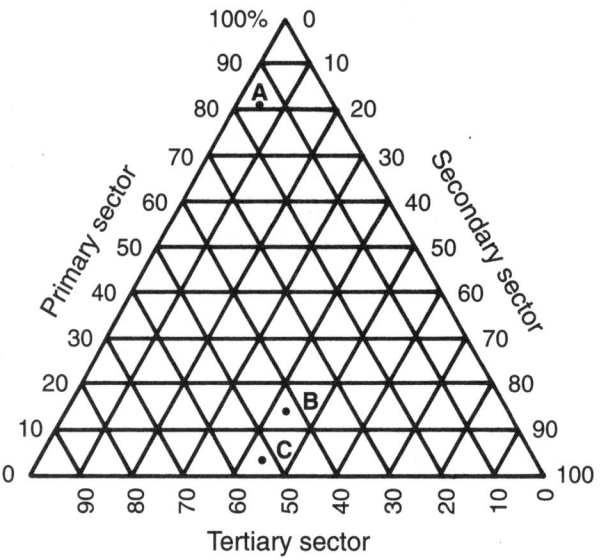

A **scatter graph** shows the relationship between two sets of geographical data. The set of data that is the cause of the other (the dependent) set is plotted along the horizontal axis.

In this case, the size of a settlement's population influences the number of services it has. The more strongly the points plotted on a scatter graph conform to a straight line, the stronger the relationship between the two sets of data.

If you need to revise this subject more thoroughly, see the relevant topics in the Letts GCSE Geography Study Guide.

Employment structures in developed and developing countries 11

QUESTIONS

1 (a) Study the table below. It shows employment structures in six countries.

1988	Percentage of workers in the		
	Primary sector %	Secondary sector %	Tertiary sector %
South Korea	20	30	50
United Kingdom	2	42	56
India	68	14	18
Ghana	54	20	26
Australia	5	33	62
Brazil	29	26	45

(i) What is meant by the:

1. Primary sector?

2. Secondary sector? (2)

(ii) Match each of these pie charts to one of the countries in the table. (2)

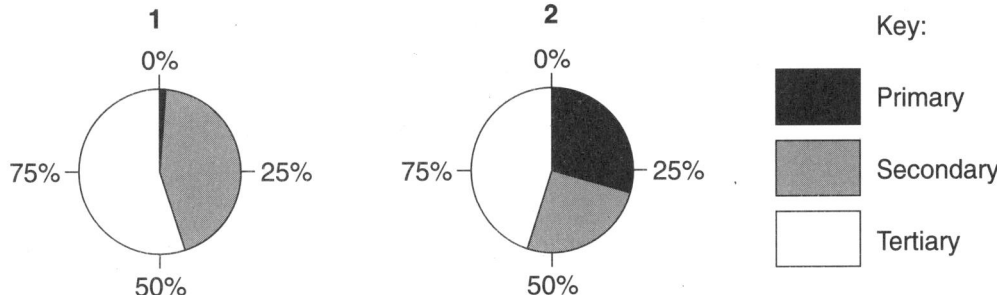

(iii) Use the information above to complete the table below. Place each of the six countries in the correct box. (3)

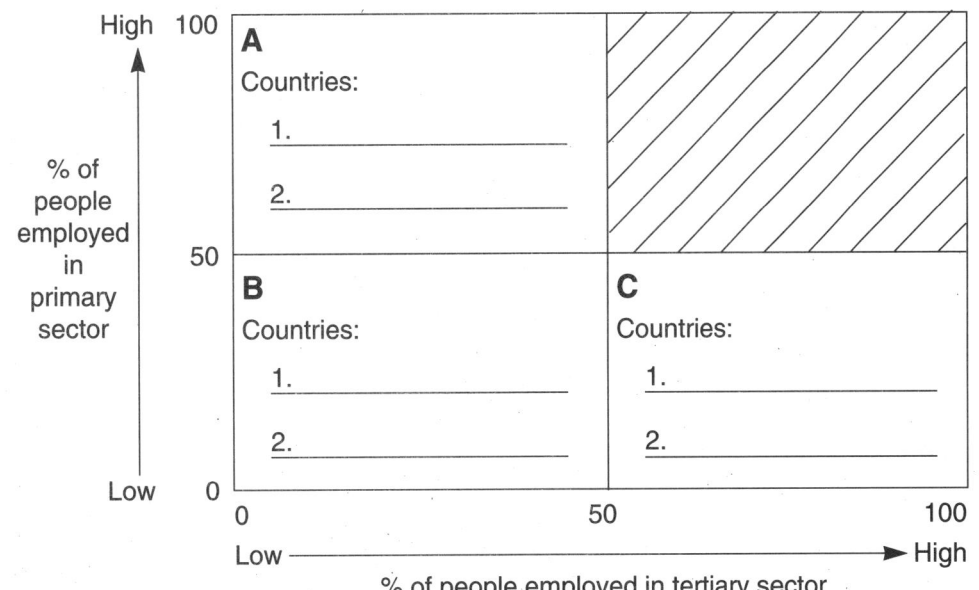

47

11 Employment structures in developed and developing countries

QUESTIONS

(iv) The boxes are labelled **A, B** and **C**. Match the letters to the statements below.

'Economically **developing** countries' =

'Economically **developed** countries' =

'Newly industrialising countries' = (1)

(v) Give **two** characteristics of economically **developing** countries. Do not write about **industry and employment structure**. (2)

(b) Study the chart below. It gives information about industrial development in South Korea.

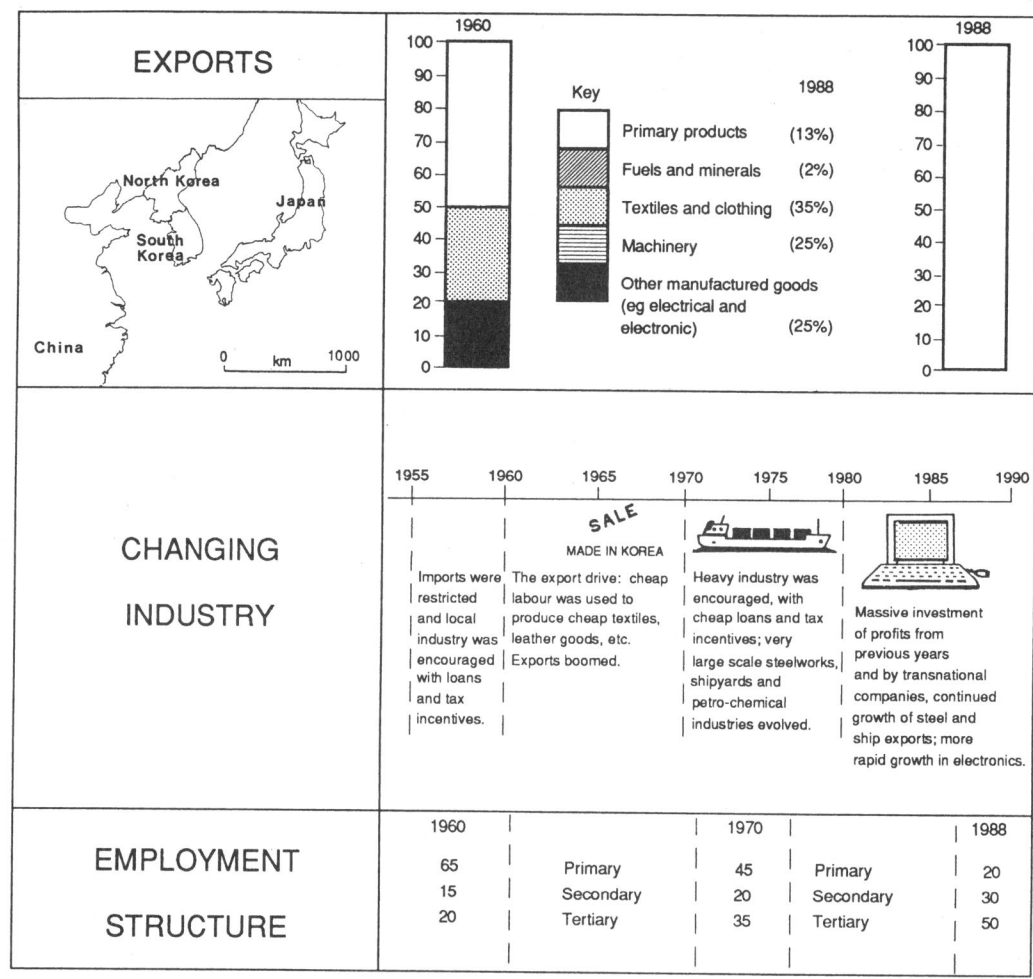

(i) Complete the graph of **exports** in 1988 (top right hand corner of chart) using the figures given in brackets on the chart above. (2)

(ii) List **two** ways in which the government encouraged the development of manufacturing. (2)

(iii) Which sector of the employment structure showed the **greatest** change between the 1960s and 1980s? (1)

(iv) Give **two** reasons to explain the changes in employment structure shown in the table. (4)

Employment structures in developed and developing countries

(v) Give **two** reasons to explain why textiles and clothing are often the first industries to be developed in an economically **developing** country. (4)

(vi) Suggest an economic and a social disadvantage which this rapid industrialisation may have brought to South Korea. (4)

(c) **Case study**

Name an area in any part of the world where **either** industry **or** agriculture has declined. Describe the reasons for the decline and the effects on the people living there.

(i) Reasons for the decline (state whether answer refers to industry **or** agriculture).

(ii) Effects on people living there. (9)

MEG/WJEC 1994

2

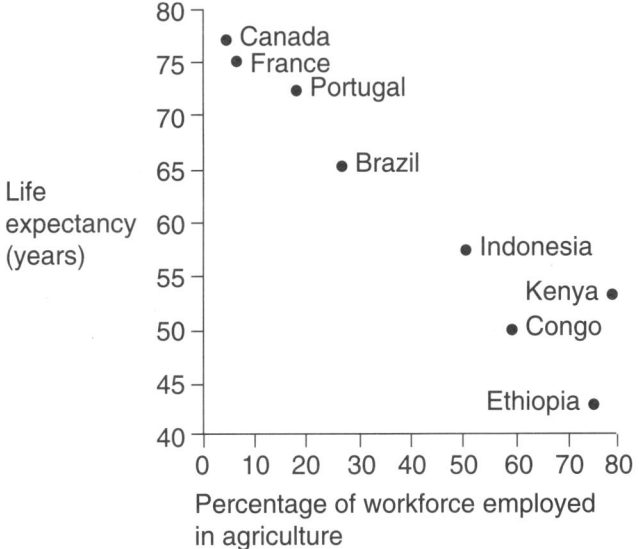

Reference diagram 1: life expectancy and percentage of workforce employed in agriculture in selected countries

(a) Look at reference diagram 1 above.

Describe the connection between life expectancy and employment in agriculture shown in the graph. (2)

(b) Explain why each of the following is a good measure of a country's level of development.

(i) Life expectancy

(ii) Percentage of workforce employed in agriculture (4)

SQA 1994

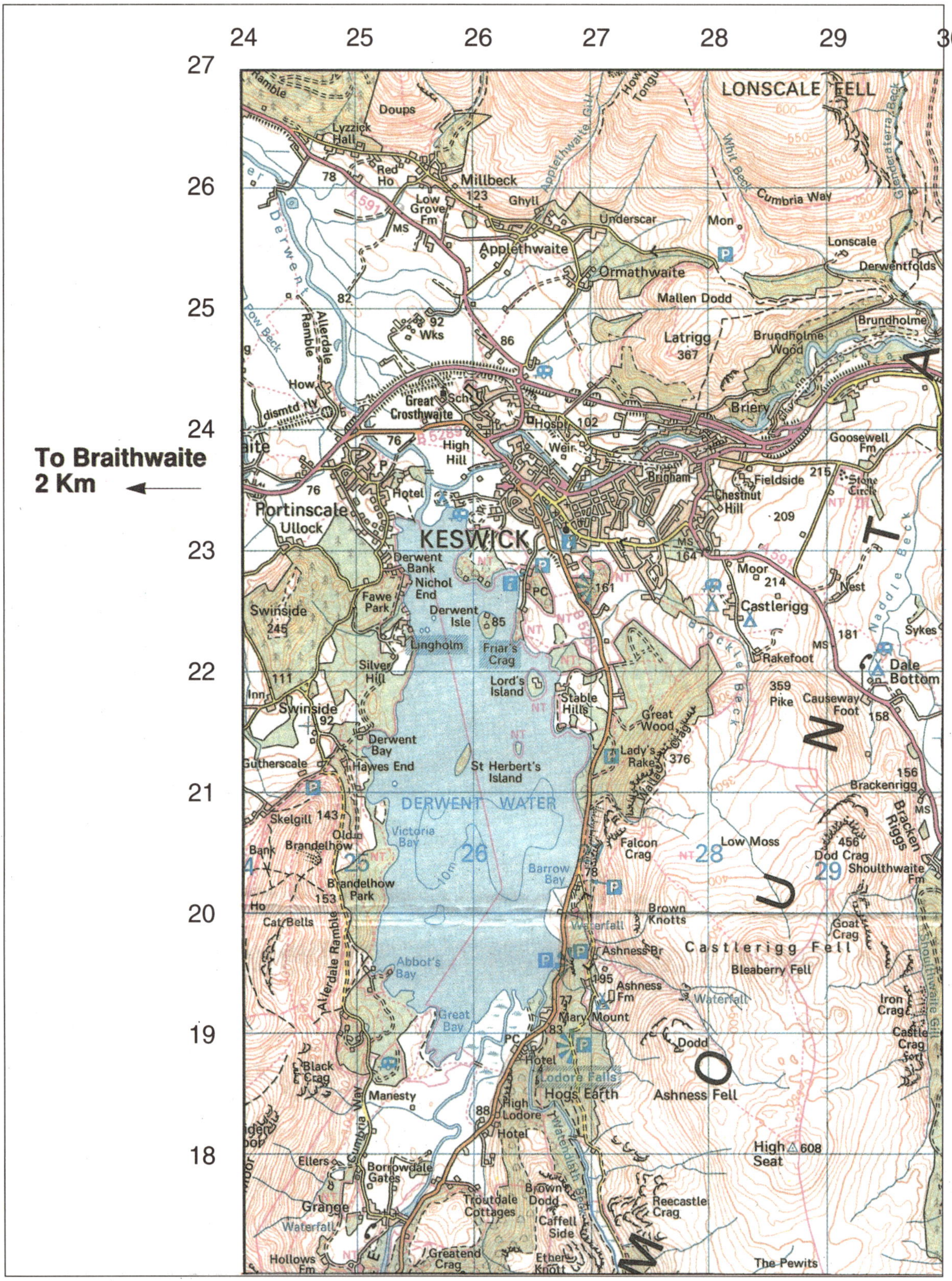

Map extract of Keswick. Scale 1:50 000.

© Crown Copyright

Resource material for Question 1 (Unit 1) pp6–7.

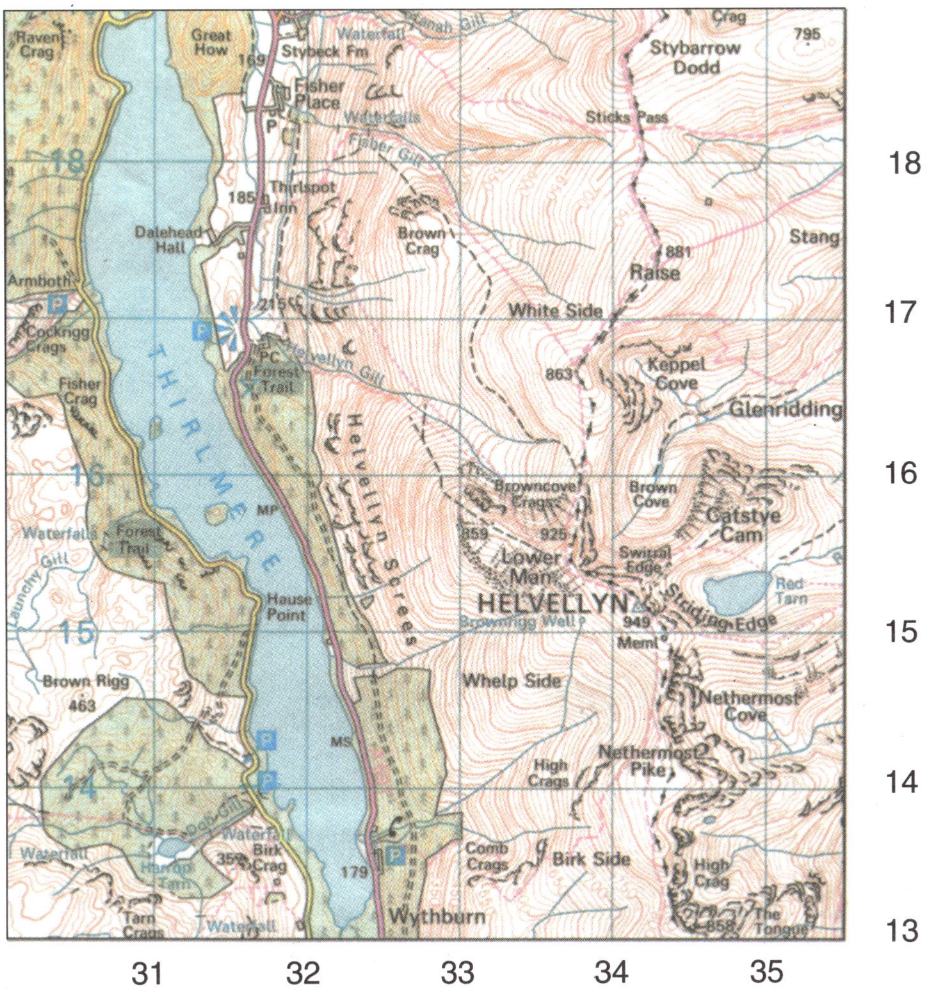

Map extract of Helvellyn. Scale 1:50 000.

Resource material for Question 1 (Unit 3) p 14.

© Crown copyright

Map extract of Milford Haven Scale 1:50 000.

Resource material for Question 1 (Unit 12) p 52

© Crown copyright

12 Mock examination paper

QUESTIONS The questions that follow are typical of current GCSE geography examinations. There are usually four questions in a full paper. *Try to complete this paper in one sitting of **one and a half hours**.*

1 Man and the environment

(a) Study the OS map extract of Milford Haven on page 51. Its scale of 1:50 000 means that 2 cm represents 1 Km.
The large oil refinery north of the village of Rhoscrowther (904022) stretches approximately 2 Km from west to east.

(i) How far does it extend from north to south? Ring the correct answer from the list below. (1)

1 Km   2 Km   4 Km   6 Km

(ii) What is the approximate area of land covered by this refinery? (1)

(iii) What is the purpose of the many jetties that appear on the map? (1)

(iv) Explain, fully, why they extend so far out from the shore. (2)

(b)

The sketch map above is an outline of the OS map extract. **On this sketch map**:

(i) Print **R** at the centre of the village of Rhoscrowther. (1)

(ii) Name the feature marked **Y**. (1)

(iii) Shade in the built-up area of the town of Milford Haven. (2)

(iv) Mark with a dotted line the route that should be taken by a tanker sailing through the Haven to discharge its oil at the refinery marked **X**. (1)

(c) Read the passage below and refer to the OS map extract and the map on the next page when answering the subsequent questions.

Mock examination paper 12

QUESTIONS

Villagers living in the shadow of an oil refinery have asked to be rehoused at a safe distance following two explosions last month.

Most of the 101 inhabitants of Rhoscrowther have petitioned the council to be moved.

The village long predates the Texaco refinery. Houses built 45 years ago on lush, open farmland are today within 200 metres of the plant. Yet 12, only, of the villagers work at the refinery.

Over the years the villagers have become accustomed to the peculiar smells and fumes from the works, even the pitting of their car bonnets has been shrugged off, but they cannot ignore these explosions.

Adapted from The Independent (Feb. 1992)

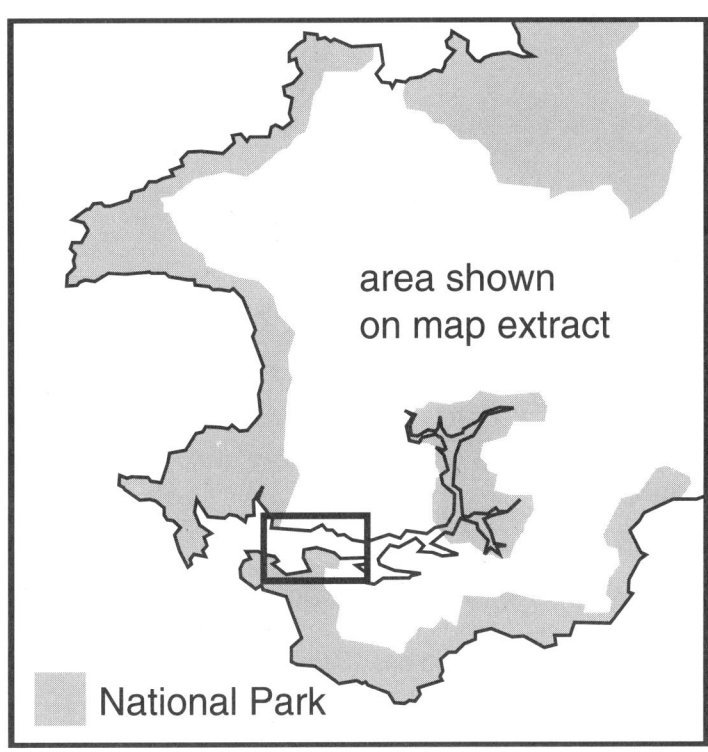

(i) What OS map evidence is there to conclude that Rhoscrowther is in the shadow of the refinery? (1)

(ii) The whole of the region shown on this OS map suffers from high unemployment. In spite of this many people in the area objected to the establishment of the refineries. From evidence **in the passage** and the map above **alone**, suggest why they objected. (5)

(iii) Describe **three** of the advantages this area possesses that persuaded the oil companies to build refineries there. (3)

(d) For any **industrial pollution** accident you have studied describe the nature of the pollution, its effects on the environment and the success of the measures taken to try and clean it up. (6)

12 Mock examination paper

QUESTIONS 2 Settlements

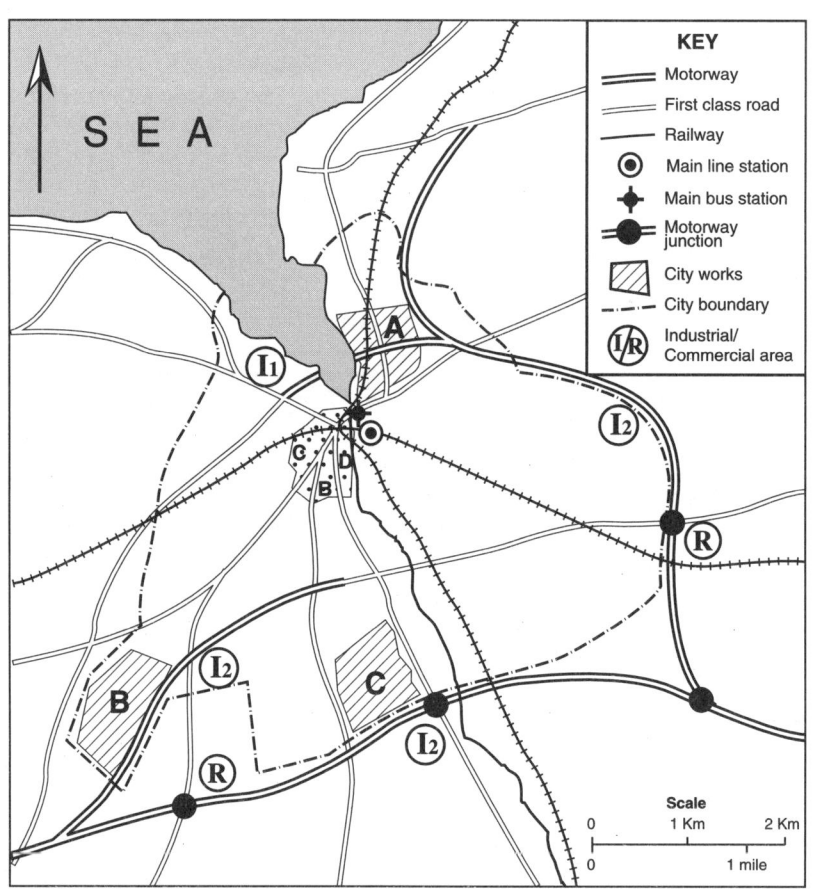

Use the map above and your own knowledge to answer the following questions.

(a) (i) This UK town first grew up because it was at the lowest bridging point on the river. Give one reason why this bridging point is important. (1)

(ii) Name four types of work characteristic of the town's CBD. (2)

(iii) Why is so much employment concentrated in the CBDs of all towns and cities. (2)

(b) **Either**
Area I_1 is occupied by a successful heavy engineering works. Describe three features of this area's geography which contribute to this success.

Or
Areas I_2 are recently built industrial estates. Factories in them make clothing, electrical goods and some hi-tech products. Describe three features of these areas' geography which have favoured their growth. (3)

(c) The two areas R are new edge-of-town retail parks.

(i) What are the advantages of these locations for the superstores being set up there? (3)

(ii) Discuss the threat these edge-of-town retail parks pose for the retailers in the CBD. Include the advantages of both locations in your discussion. (5)

Mock examination paper

(d)

Wards	% households with no car	% population unemployed	% population under 15	% ethnic minority	Accommodation Tenure %		
					owner occupied	council or association rented	privately rented
A	41	11	17	18	48	23	29
B	36	9	20	8	39	57	4
C	5	6	13	1	91	3	6

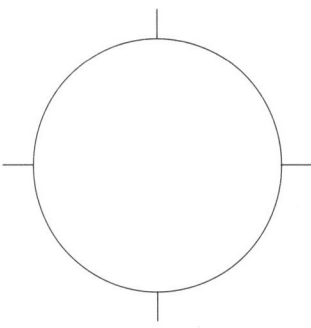

(i) Show and label on the divided circle above the accommodation tenure for Ward A. (2)

(ii) 23%, 14% and 12% are the percentages of the population 65 years old and over in the three wards. In which of the wards do you judge the 23% to live? Explain your answer. (1)

(iii) Using all the information you have been given, state which of the three wards you think has the best quality of life. Justify your answer. (6)

3 Population

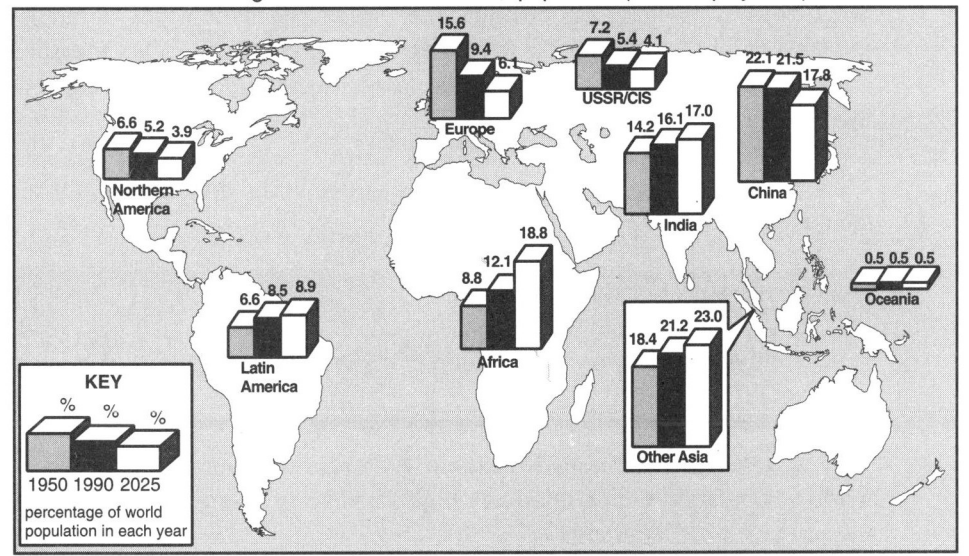

Changing share of world population
Percentage distribution of the world's population (medium projection)

12 Mock examination paper

QUESTIONS

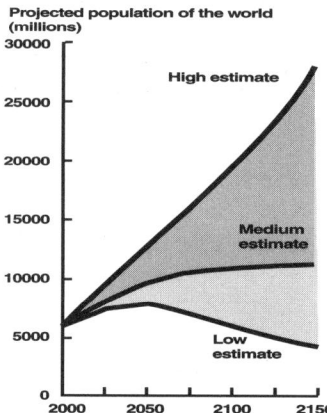

Projected population

Study the figures above and on the previous page.

(a) (i) Which area of the world named on the map contained the highest percentage of the world's population in 1990?

  (ii) Which area of the world is predicted to show no change in its percentage share of world population by 2025?

  (iii) The projected population graph shows a wide variation. Give one reason why the estimates vary so much. (4)

(b) (i) What is the common feature of the trends shown in the four graphs for the regions in the developing world (excluding China)? (1)

  (ii) Give three reasons to explain this trend. (3)

  (iii) What are the implications for the people of the developing world if this prediction proves to be accurate? (3)

  (iv) Some people believe that controlling the world's population growth rate is the most important task facing the international community. What measures could be taken by the international community to slow down the predicted rate of increase? (4)

(c) (i) What is the common feature of the trends shown in the three graphs for regions in the developed world? (1)

  (ii) Give two reasons to explain this trend. (2)

  (iii) What are the implications for the people of Europe if this predicted trend proves to be accurate? (3)

  (iv) Why was Europe (excluding Russia) in 1950 able to support nearly 16% of the world's population with a relatively high standard of living though comprising only 4% of the world's land area? (4)

56

Answers

1 THE WATER CYCLE AND RIVERS AND THEIR VALLEYS

| Question | Answer | Mark |

1 (a) (i)

Examiner's tip Once you realise that evaporation is the conversion of water from a liquid into a gas – water vapour, which rises from the surface of the land (see vertical arrow on diagram) – the sequence of the next three processes is clear.

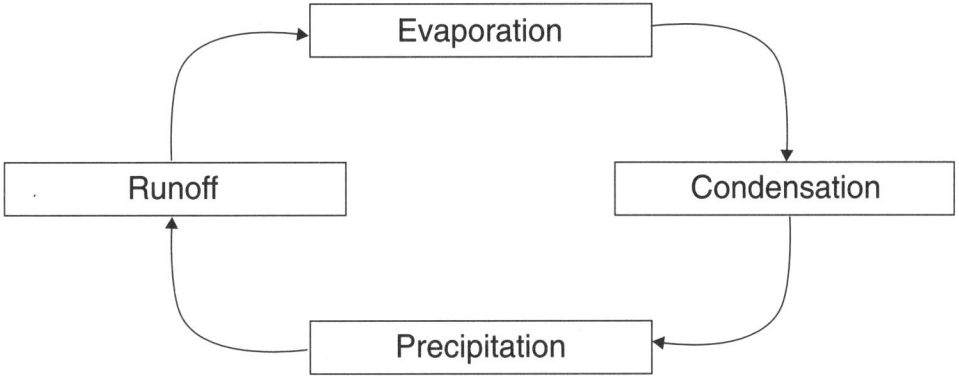

1

(ii) Transpiration 1

(iii) Because it is warmer in summer and higher temperatures lead to greater transpiration.
Alternatively, because there are more leaves on the trees in summer. 1

(iv) Water table 1

(b)

Examiner's tip This involves you in a study of an OS map extract. Make sure you are aware of the policy of your examination group. Will a key for all the symbols used on the map be supplied to you in the examination, or will you be expected to know them?

(i) A confluence 1

(ii) The main features of the River Derwent are: a general NNW course; a very gentle gradient along the river; some meanders just after its exit from the lake for about 1 km; all its tributaries enter from the east; an ox bow lake. 3

(iii)

Examiner's tip When the phrase 'using map evidence only' is used in a question, it means just that. There is no point in including in your answer details that you have learned in class or from a textbook, if they are not evident on the map.

This is a lacustrine (lake) delta. It is an area of flat land, extending into the lake and it is quite marshy. The river flows through the middle of it. 3

Answers to Unit 1

Question		Answer	Mark
	(iv)	The River Derwent carries a large load (since it has just left the mountains). The velocity of the river water is checked as it flows into the lake. This leads to a loss of energy by the river. It is forced to deposit its load.	3
(c)	(i)	Many river valleys have a flat floor which may be even lower than the river itself. When the river overflows, this flat land (flood plain) is flooded and the water has difficulty in returning to the river even when the river stops overflowing. The river bed may have risen through the river depositing its load on it, so there is less room for the river to rise before overflowing.	2
	(ii)	The channel may be dredged, so it is made deeper to take more water. The material obtained through dredging may be piled up on the river banks to make a more effective barrier to flooding. (Alternatively, you could mention that straightening the river's course increases the velocity of the river, making flooding less likely.)	2
(d)	(i)	(Name *one*) Ox bow lake or cut off (A) *OR* levee (B)	1
	(ii)		

Examiner's tip You cannot be expected to draw this cross-section to scale as the line X–Y provided is more than four times the distance on the diagram.

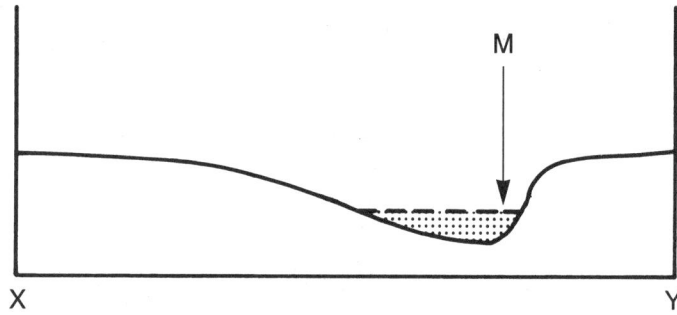

2

(iii)

Examiner's tip Feature A is chosen here because, though an ox bow lake is a feature of little significance, it is popular with examiners as both river erosion and deposition occur in its formation. Usually one would use an annotated diagram when describing its formation.

Answers to Unit 2

Question	Answer	Mark

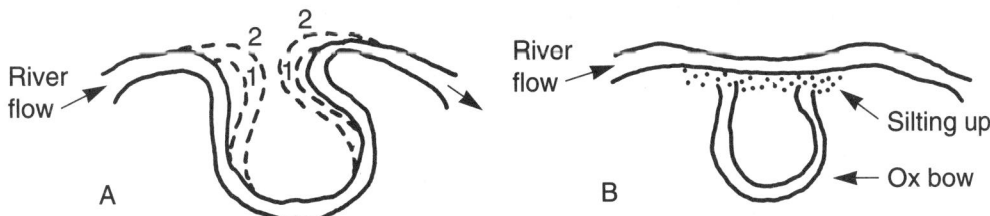

Because the river flows more quickly on the outside of the bend, erosion through undercutting will take place there. This is seen in diagram A above where the neck of the meander is attacked from both outside bends to position 1, then to position 2. Then during a time of flood the river will break through, short circuiting the loop (diagram B). Silting will take place along the new river course so that the meander loop is permanently cut off, becoming an ox bow lake. **4**

2 COASTS

Question	Answer	Mark

1 (a)

> **Examiner's tip**
> Ensure that you match up the map and the aerial photograph accurately. Matching the railway routes and the tide on the photograph with High Water Mark will help you do this.

(i) X = Hoverport   Y = Richborough Power Station

(ii) Ferry terminal; golf course; residential area; farmland.

(iii) There is no sand or mud visible. **7**

(b)

> **Examiner's tip**
> Read Fig. 2 very carefully. If you do, you will find that together with Fig. 1 and the photograph you can answer all parts of (b) and (c) from the data supplied.

(i) 1. They intend creating wildlife sanctuaries on the artificial islands.
2. They intend to retain existing beaches.

(ii) Hoverport

(iii) To shelter the recreational basin from strong waves or severe weather.

(iv) 1. It will be safer for dinghy sailing as it will be protected from the weather.

Answers to Unit 2

2. It will be possible to use the basin whatever the state of the tide.   6

(c)

> **Examiner's tip**
> This is an example of the now well established type of question where you as a candidate are expected to put yourself into the mind of a third party, in this case a resident of Cliffsend. This should not be too difficult, as there is plenty of information in Fig. 2.

(i) 1. The new recreational/leisure facilities will be available to them if they become members.
2. New retail outlets will be built on their doorstep.
3. The beaches are safeguarded.
OR There will be less noise if the hoverport is removed.
OR Some employment openings may be created.

(ii) A big increase in traffic flow is likely so there will be more noise and air pollution.   4

(d)

> **Examiner's tip**
> Here you will have to draw upon any case study of coastal pollution you have made. Note that the question uses the present and the past tense, 'is' and 'has been'. So if you write about a situation that existed 5 or even 20 years ago, you will certainly satisfy the question's requirements. Again, there is no scale requirement. You could write about pollution in the Mediterranean or in a small British river estuary.

(i) Named area = Croyde Bay, North Devon

This very attractive bay has had an increasingly serious problem during the past ten years or so. **Sewage** that is taken out to sea by pipeline is returned to the beach by waves and tides. The local sewage system is unable to cope with the increased load brought about by the vast increase in caravan/tenting holidays. In addition there has been a significant increase in **litter** pollution as gift shops and cafes have opened for the tourists. Some further pollution is brought here by longshore drift from the coast to the south while, occasionally, traces of **oil** pollution occur from ships illegally cleaning out their tanks at sea. Finally, even the magnificent backing sand dunes have been defiled by damaging walking and the picking of unusual plant species.

(ii) There needs to be a modern sewage treatment plant which will return sewage to the sea in an almost clear liquid form. Given sufficient investment this could be done. Certainly the outfall pipe needs to be extended far out to sea so that the sewage is dispersed well away from the coast. For litter, more bins could be provided and/or penalties increased. The dunes have been fenced off with clear warning and explanatory notices to visitors.   8

Answers to Unit 3

3 WEATHERING AND GLACIATION

Question	Answer	Mark

1 (a)

Examiner's tip: Be sure to bring both photograph and map together in your mind. You must match the landforms on the two to determine the direction in which the camera was pointing. Look at the shape of the lake Red Tarn. The more irregular western edge of the lake on the map is top left on the photograph. Keppel Cove, which is NNW of Red Tarn on the map, is towards the top right of the photograph; that is, the whole photograph is swivelled to the right, thus the camera was pointing north-west.

    (i)   A = Glenridding, B = Helvellyn, C = Striding Edge   3

    (ii)   C   1

Examiner's tip: Remember, an arête is a knife-edged ridge.

    (iii)   Thirlmere   1

(b)   (i)   D = Biological   E = Chemical   F = Physical (or freeze/thaw)   3

Examiner's tip: Clearly, the examiner will be looking for three different processes.

    (ii)   Freeze/thaw or Physical   1

Examiner's tip: Remember that, though very cold, there was some melting during the day if the snow/ice surface faced the sun.

    (iii)   Scree

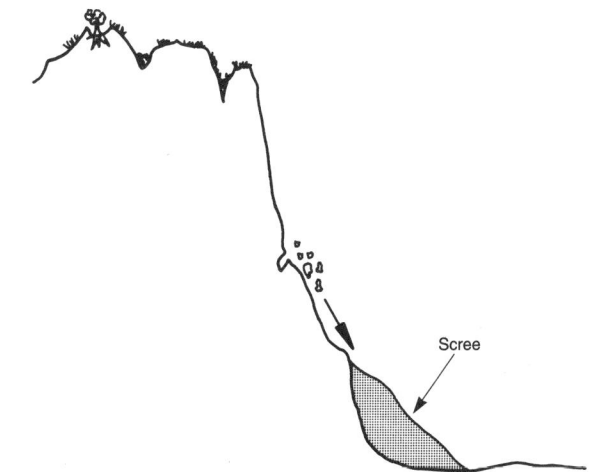

Answers to Unit 3

Question	Answer	Mark

(c) (i)

Examiner's tip — Three full descriptions of features are suggested for three marks.

The sides and back wall of the corrie are very steep and high, rising to over 900 m in places. These steep slopes are very rocky with some scree developments. The corrie is deepest in the centre, which has filled with water creating a lake.

3

(ii)

Examiner's tip — You are told to use at least two diagrams. Make sure you do, otherwise you will lose some marks. If you annotate the diagrams fully there is no need for separate text.

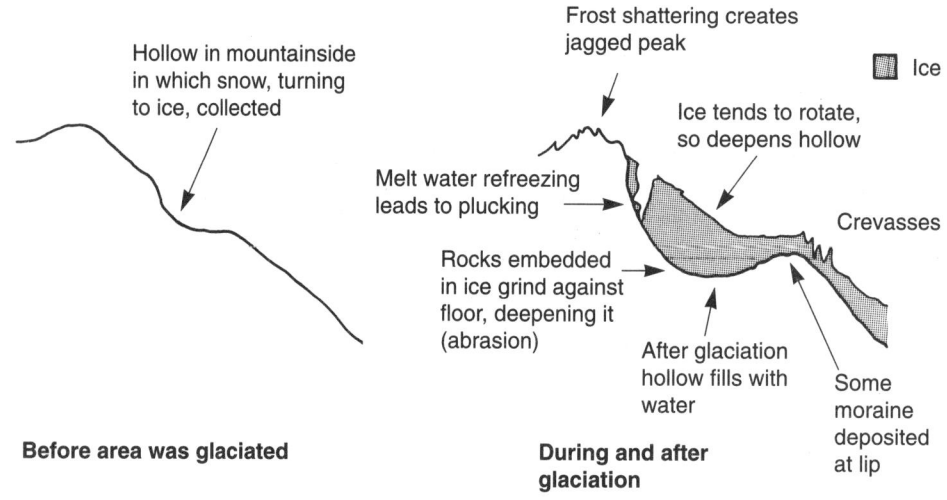

Before area was glaciated — Hollow in mountainside in which snow, turning to ice, collected

During and after glaciation — Frost shattering creates jagged peak; Ice tends to rotate, so deepens hollow; Melt water refreezing leads to plucking; Rocks embedded in ice grind against floor, deepening it (abrasion); Crevasses; After glaciation hollow fills with water; Some moraine deposited at lip

6

(d) (i)

Examiner's tip — The question states **at least** three reasons. Presumably, this means that a simple, undeveloped reason will gain one mark, a developed one up to two marks. So three full reasons or six bare reasons will give full marks. Below are six full reasons.

- This region is popular with walkers all year round so the path surface and its original vegetation has little respite from walking boots. Once worn away the vegetation finds it difficult to regrow.
- The prevailing low temperatures and harsh winds slow down growth.
- The poor soils, if not compacted by walkers, are eroded away by the heavy rainfall of the region.
- There is rapid runoff since some paths are on the knife-edge of ridges.
- Freeze/thaw is rampant because at this height the temperature during the night is often below freezing and this helps to break up the paths.
- Many of these regions are National Parks which encourage visitors.

6

Answers to Unit 4

Question	Answer	Mark
(ii)	Appeals can be made to walkers to redirect their steps. In severe cases of erosion walkers can be banned from the area. The ground may be covered with wire mesh to lessen the impact of feet and allow regeneration of vegetation. Water may be encouraged to move laterally through concrete grooving so reducing run off. Paths may be walled up to prevent their collapse.	4

4 WEATHER AND CLIMATE

Question	Answer	Mark

1 (a)

> **Examiner's tip**
> You are referred to a map showing the location of the world's equatorial rain forests, and to four climate graphs.
> The world map includes latitude lines. These, clearly, are there to help you in your answers. The climate graphs show temperature and rainfall. Remember that on such graphs temperature is shown by a line, rainfall by columns. **Do not confuse them**. The graphs in this example are not printed on graph paper. So make sure, when making calculations, that you have a straight edge which you place absolutely horizontally to read the temperature and rainfall values from the scales. Again, note that the height of these four stations above sea level is given. Pay attention to this. It does not matter too much in this question, but increased altitude means lower temperatures (1 °C lower for every 150 m of altitude) and often higher rainfall.

(i)	All the Equatorial Rain Forests are located within the Tropics. Most are located within 5° latitude of the Equator: in South America (the Amazon Basin), central Africa (the Congo Basin) and in south-east Asia.	3
(ii)	300 mm	1
(iii)	These are regions of high temperatures, so every day the heated ground heats the air above it. This rises, cools to condensation point, clouds form and heavy rain falls. (This is convectional rain.) Water vapour is added to the air through evaporation over the nearby seas before the air moves over the land. The luxuriant vegetation also adds lots of water vapour to the air through the process of transpiration.	3
(iv)	This is the difference in value between the highest and lowest mean monthly temperatures.	2
(v)	It is small because the Sun is **always** high in the sky and because night and day are equal in length throughout the year, so there is little variation in heat received.	2

Answers to Unit 4

Question	Answer	Mark
(b) (i)	Millibars	1

Examiner's tip This involves you in a study of a weather map. Some examination groups will give you a key for the symbols used on the map. Other groups will expect you to learn the symbols, and indeed may ask you questions that specifically test your knowledge of the symbols. Make sure that you are aware of the policy of your examination group.

(ii)	An anticyclone or high	1
(iii)		

Examiner's tip A common error made by candidates is to confuse wind direction. Remember winds are named after the direction they blow **from** e.g. a south or southerly wind blows **from** the south.

	(A) Isobars are far apart *OR* The pressure gradient is slack	1
	(B) Southern Britain has high pressure to the south-east and low pressure to the north-west. Winds blow around the high in a clockwise direction and slightly out, hence the southerly winds over southern Britain.	3
(c)		

Examiner's tip As with all questions when you have to read a passage, make sure you read it right through to gain an overview before you return to particular phrases or sentences that relate to specific questions. Also, note the date of the weather map; it is a **winter** chart.

(i)	(A) Nitrogen dioxide	1
	(B) Asthma, coughing and other chest ailments	1
(ii)	The air is fairly still so there is no wind to disperse pollutants. Air in a winter high is stable and cold and is subsiding, so it traps pollutants near the ground. Air comes in from the nearby continent bringing in pollutants.	2
(iii)	Because cars are the main source of pollution such as nitrogen dioxide through their exhaust emissions. Alternative transport, such as train, tube or bus, creates much less air pollution in total as one engine carries many more passengers.	4

2 (a)

Examiner's tip Once you have matched up the labels on the satellite image with their corresponding locations on the weather map, this question becomes a straightforward test of accurate symbol/isobaric map recognition.

Answers to Unit 4

Question	Answer	Mark
(i)	A = Depression B = Warm front C = Cold front D = Occlusion E = Ridge	5

(ii)

> **Examiner's tip** — Compare carefully the position of the black line (B) on the image and the warm front on the map. Remember a warm front has the main body of thick cloud **ahead** of its surface location.

The line runs through the Shetlands and eastern North Sea on the image but almost touches the north-east coast of Scotland and runs through the western North Sea on the map. The front on the image is ahead of the main body of cloud near the Shetlands.   **2**

(iii) Winds blow anticlockwise around a low so they blow from the east and north-east near F. Thus, clouds spiral round the centre of the low. (Technically the cloud is linked to a backbent occlusion.)   **2**

(iv) Temperature 4°C; 6 oktas of cloud; rain shower; WNW wind; wind speed force 5 (or 23–27 knots); air pressure between 988 and 992 mb.   **3**

(v) Patchy white shadings denote shower clouds. It lies behind the cold front hence lower temperatures.   **2**

(b)

> **Examiner's tip** — You must explain. Note the date – winter, and the time – night.

(i) P = 5°C as it is fairly far south but in the middle of a ridge with clear skies and calm conditions. It has been dark for 9 or more hours so much nocturnal radiation. Chilled air has collected near the cold ground. There is no wind to disperse it so a temperature inversion occurs.

(ii) Q = 10°C because it is in the warm sector, and is therefore influenced by mild tropical maritime air. The cloud cover and strong winds prevent significant radiation.

(iii) R = 4°C because it is behind the cold front. The strong winds from the north-west quarter bring polar maritime air.   **6**

(c) (i)

> **Examiner's tip** — You now have to compare two weather maps 24 hours apart. When studying the depression think of pressure, closeness of isobars, any directional movement of the centre or the fronts, and squeezing of the warm sector.

The depression has deepened greatly, the pressure at the centre falling from 972 to below 944 mb. As a result the isobars are now much closer together (the pressure gradient has steepened). The centre has moved more than 500 km to the north-east. Fronts have swept eastwards reducing the size of the warm sector.   **4**

Answers to Unit 4

Question	Answer	Mark

(ii)

Examiner's tip
The map provides you with little information other than that the British Isles are in the cold sector of a depression with strong WNW or NW air flow – very strong over Scotland, least strong over south-east England, plus, of course, the fact that it is winter and 3 a.m. You must use your meteorological expertise. Use any two of the following three points.

Over most of the British Isles it is very windy, especially so in Scotland. This is because of the very steep pressure gradient, with about 50 mb difference in air pressure between Cornwall and the Shetlands.

There will be showers, as any polar maritime air mass will be unstable. Showers will be frequent over western coasts and hills as air is forced to rise.

Almost certainly the precipitation will be wintry over high ground, for temperatures fall with altitude at 1°C per 150 m, and this air mass is cold at this time of year.

6

5 POPULATION AND RESOURCES

Question	Answer	Mark

1 (a)

Examiner's tip
The type of diagrams you are asked to study here are common in population questions. Remember that they show three features of the population: (i) its age structure, (ii) the male/female balance and (iii) the total size of the population.

(i) An official count of the population of a country. In Britain censuses are taken every ten years.

1

(ii)

Examiner's tip
Note that the question states 'ways' so at least **two** similarities need to be mentioned.

Both graphs are widest at the base and become progressively narrower as one moves up the age ranges. In short, they are both triangular and symmetrical.

2

(iii)

Examiner's tip
There are three marks available so give three changes.

Answers to Unit 5

Question	Answer	Mark

The pyramid has changed from a triangular to a more pillar-like shape. The bulge in the middle shows that there were many more middle-aged people in 1988 than in 1891. The much wider top shows a big increase in the number of elderly people. The total population shown by the pyramid has increased considerably.   **3**

(iv) The big increase in the number of people over 60 years of age means that:

- much more state money has to be spent on retirement pensions – hence moves to raise the pension age of women,

- more and more has to be spent on medical care in hospitals and nursing homes for the elderly,

- more welfare services such as 'home helps' and 'meals on wheels' are needed.

All of this has to be provided by a working population between 20 and 60 years of age which forms a much smaller proportion of the total population than before – while many of this group are unemployed. Will they be able to continue paying towards pensions and medical services?   **4**

(v)

Examiner's tip
Answers here can be based on religious objections, economic objections and on objections that population controls limit the rights of the individual.

Some people believe that controlling population growth is acting against God's will. The Roman Catholic church, for example, is opposed to artificial methods of contraception. Many more people are opposed to abortion, which they regard as tantamount to murder, while most people in this country disagree with infanticide, a measure which has been employed in China to control population numbers. Subsistence farmers in India are opposed to population controls as they need lots of children to work on their farms and to support them in their old age.   **3**

(b) (i) Population density is the number of people per unit area.   **1**

(ii)

Examiner's tip
You need to study Fig. 4 to answer this question. It is not a very clear map. Make sure you find the correct column base before measuring the column's length.

Bangladesh   **1**

(iii) Population density figures are more useful than total population figures as they tell you how crowded a country is. If you know about the country's economy, including whether farming or industry predominates, you can conclude whether it is overpopulated or underpopulated or neither.   **2**

Answers to Unit 5

Question	Answer	Mark
(iv)		

Examiner's tip This is the most important sub-question comprising almost one third of the total marks. Make sure you understand the word 'physical'. It is often taken to be those aspects of geography which are not 'human', e.g. relief, altitude, geology, soils and climate **but** this can vary. Check the syllabus for your exam on this matter. The command words 'comment on' are rather vague. Take them to mean 'write explanatory notes' on. Again, this question states 'with reference to places' so at least two must be chosen and named. Choose one sparsely and one densely populated area if you can.

Very few people live in Tibet because it is so high and inaccessible. Much of it is a high plateau over 3500 m above sea level, but there are deep valleys and raging rivers. This means that farming is very difficult. The high altitude leads to temperatures too low for crops to grow. Winds are often strong, so the thin soils are often blown away. Because Tibet is north of the Himalayas precipitation is low, again too low for successful farming, so the land has a low carrying capacity for humans and livestock. To build roads in this country is difficult and expensive. Steep slopes have to be overcome, bridges built and tunnels made. Roads can be blocked by fallen rocks. All this makes it unattractive for human settlement.

Not too far away from Tibet is the lower Ganges Valley. Here population density is very high. People have been attracted here because the land is low and flat so it is easy to farm and easy to build roads on. The low altitude leads to higher temperatures (over 20°C for much of the year), while every year the monsoon brings rain. This land is part of the Ganges flood plain, with soils which are alluvial and fertile. They are underlain by impermeable rock and will retain standing irrigation water. So this is an excellent region for growing rice, perhaps two crops a year. This will maintain a high density of population. **8**

6 THE URBAN WORLD

Question	Answer	Mark
1		

Examiner's tip The first part of this question asks you to study a model. Models are frequently used in geography, especially when studying the urban world.

(a) (i) A=2 B=1 C=3 D=4   **4**
    (ii)

Examiner's tip You are asked for a description rather than a list. Note that there are six marks so you must mention the feature plus a development point to gain full marks.

1. There are many shops which are often found in covered arcades or pedestrianised streets.
2. Land is expensive so buildings are tall. This creates more office space.

Answers to Unit 6

	3. All routes converge on the city centre so the narrow streets often become congested.	6
(iii)	CBD/City Centre	1
(iv)	Ways of easing traffic congestion in towns include: • encouraging people to use public transport by making fares cheaper and giving priority to buses in towns. • Introducing park and ride schemes which reduces the number of cars coming into the town centre. • Traffic management measures such as one-way systems, tidal flows and traffic lights which are designed to increase traffic flow.	5

(b)

> **Examiner's tip** Be careful. There is a lot of information to consider before answering. Make sure you justify your choice using Fig. 2.

(i)	Statement P: ward D, which is close to the edge of the city, has over 60% of its households owner occupied whereas ward A, which is close to the city centre, has less than 20% owner occupied housing.	4
(ii)		

> **Examiner's tip** Two developed reasons are needed for full marks.

	Ward A is in the inner city. Here residents tend to be poorer than those living in ward D so they cannot afford cars. There is less need for cars in ward A as it is better served with public transport and people can walk to the city centre as it is much closer.	4

(c) (i)

> **Examiner's tip** A change of emphasis in the question. This is now about shopping rather than housing. Again there is a lot of information to take in before answering the question. Note the title at the top of each graph.

People are prepared to travel further to use the superstore. More people travel to the superstore by car. Fewer people walk to the superstore. People travel to the High Street using more varied forms of transport. No one travels to the superstore by train or tube.	6

(ii)

> **Examiner's tip** Here you are asked to describe and explain. This means that you have to say what is there and how or why it got there.

Many people can walk to the village store as the store serves the local community. Most shoppers travel less than 2 Km and no one travels more than 7 Km. This is because village stores sell convenience goods such as bread and milk so people are less likely to make long journeys in order to purchase these goods.	6

Answers to Unit 7

Question	Answer	Mark
(iii)		

Examiner's tip Three marks are available for each part of the answer so make sure you attempt both. Do not be confused by the use of the word 'superstore' (as opposed to out-of-town shopping centres as mentioned in the question). For the purpose of this question assume that they are one and the same thing.

City centre stores could suffer a loss of business, so income would fall and may lead to closure. The city centre becomes less busy so reducing congestion and pollution. City centres have been forced to redevelop in order to compete with out-of-town stores.

Valuable land may be used up and prime agricultural land lost. Other stores may be attracted to the area causing the site to expand. There will be an increase in traffic which leads to greater congestion and more pollution. It creates jobs for suburban dwellers particularly parents looking for part-time work. **6**

7 URBANISATION

Question	Answer	Mark
1 (a)		

Examiner's tip This is a straightforward question, but measure the bars carefully when answering (iii).

    (i) 22 millions

    (ii) Natural increase

    (iii) 1971-81   **3**

(b)   **4**

Examiner's tip You will need to draw three flow lines. So, with a scale of .75 mm to 3%, Rajastan's flow line will be 1.5 mm wide, that for Gujarat 3.75 mm, that for Uttar Pradesh 3 mm. Make sure you draw the flow lines neatly, pointing of course, at Bombay.

(c)   (i) Greater

    (ii) The further away the migrant's home the greater the cost to get to Bombay. The greater the distance from Bombay the more likely it is that other large cities will be nearer and attract possible migrants.

    (iii)

Examiner's tip You are looking for a state which is far away from Bombay but which sends a high percentage of migrants to the city.

Uttar Pradesh

Answers to Unit 7

Question	Answer	Mark

Examiner's tip Since you are trying to explain why more people move out from this state you are looking for push factors. You cannot be expected to possess knowledge specific to this state. Use your own general geographical knowledge to answer.

(iv) 1. There have been severe floods or drought which have caused famine forcing people out.
2. Perhaps this state is more overpopulated than others, causing greater poverty and disease. (Other push factors could be civil war, changes in farming methods.) — **6**

(d) (i) An island

(ii)

Examiner's tip You are asked to use Fig. 3. Remember Fig. 3 includes both a map and a key. Presumably there are three marks for this part of the question, so make three points.

No growth will be allowed within the existing city of Bombay. Elsewhere on the island, within the greater Bombay boundary, restricted growth will be allowed at specific points. Major growth will take place at a new Bombay city on the mainland. (An alternative could be: growth will take place in an arc of small centres mostly on the mainland, within the Bombay region boundary.) — **4**

(e)

Examiner's tip You may choose a city anywhere outside the UK. However, the material below relates to a city in the Economically Developing World. Make sure you name the city. Choose a city that you have studied; São Paulo, Mexico City, Calcutta, Nairobi, are popular examples. There are eight marks for this question so develop your answer fully.

São Paulo

(i) There are many problems. The city has spread widely using up fertile farmland on some of which intensive market gardening used to take place. The population increase has outstripped the city's ability to provide jobs so there is much unemployment. There is insufficient housing to cater for immigrants so overcrowding and disease are rife. There has been an overload on all public services such as medical facilities, schools, electricity, sewerage and water supply. On the city outskirts shanty towns have grown up which have all the problems mentioned above to an extreme degree.

(ii) São Paulo's city planners are trying to tackle the shanty town problems in a more enlightened way. Once they used to demolish the favelas only for them to reappear somewhere else. Now they give legal tenure to some of the shanty town dwellers. This encourages them to improve the shacks themselves, replacing cardboard, plastic and metal with breeze blocks and mortar. Some go on to open small businesses. The city authorities provide water, sewerage and electricity supplies. Some shanty towns have been improved

Answers to Unit 7

so much that they are now classed as a periferia (suburb). Efforts are also being made to improve the city's public transport system. This will allow the unemployed of the shanty towns to travel farther to work. More funds are being directed into clinics and schools to deal with the large numbers of children.	8

8 AGRICULTURE

Question	Answer	Mark

1

> **Examiner's tip** This is an unusual type of climate graph with which you may be unfamiliar, so take care. Note that the circular lines indicating 20°C (not marked on the scale) and 10°C are slightly heavier than the others.

(a)	(i)	July 12°C	1
	(ii)		

> **Examiner's tip** Need for irrigation water is greatest when it is warm and dry, then evaporation is higher and crops are growing fastest.

		December, January, February	1
	(iii)	1. These months are the driest and warmest so there is high evaporation. 2. Plants have the greatest need for water then.	2
	(iv)		

> **Examiner's tip** Note this graph is for a place in the southern hemisphere. You can tell this because December and January are the warmest months.

		Summer	1
(b)	(i)	South	1
	(ii)	100 and 200	1
	(iii)		

> **Examiner's tip** The question asks about Lourensford Plantation – this is the name of the fruit farm. Do not confuse it with the plantation shown in the cross-section.

This fruit farm is higher above sea level than Cape Town, so temperatures will be lower because of its increased altitude. The farm faces south and is backed by a steep slope so, as it is in the southern hemisphere, it will be in the shade for much of the time.		3

Answers to Unit 8

(c) (i) The furrows and underground pipes.   **1**

(ii)

Examiner's tip   Note the phrase 'in full' in the question.

The Lourens River is a lot lower than the orchards, so river water would have to be pumped uphill to irrigate the orchards. This would be costly and would reduce profits.   **2**

(iii) Any three of the following: to stop soil erosion; to prevent rock falls from above causing damage below; as a source of money from timber sales (diversification); to slow down any silting up of the irrigation channels.   **3**

(d)

Examiner's tip   Remember your example must be taken from an MEDC.

(i) Name of country: Britain – a dairy farm.

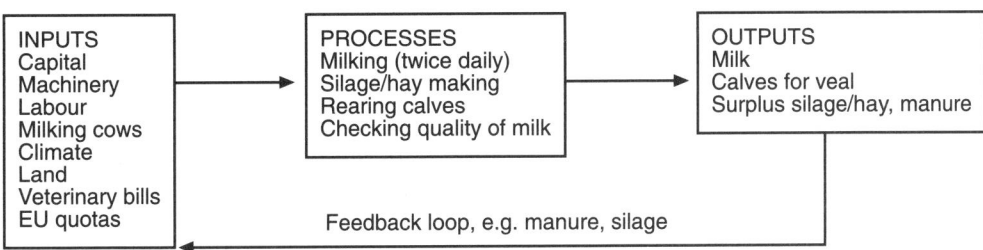

    4

(ii) The farmer chooses to practise dairy farming because:

1. The farm is on level land – the cattle are not overexerted by moving about.

2. The farm has clay soils – these give lush grass growth and so promote a good milk yield.

3. The farm has mild winters – this allows grass to grow for most of the year and so less feedstuff needs to be provided; this means that cattle need not be brought indoors frequently, so costs are reduced.

4. Grants from UK and EU government agencies have encouraged the purchase of sophisticated machinery for milking, refrigeration and storage.

5. This farmer has bought up a neighbour's milk quota, so the farm can sell all the milk produced.

6. There is a reliable market for milk nearby. The milk is collected by refrigerated Milk Marque tankers.

    5

Answers to Unit 9

9 MANUFACTURING INDUSTRY

Question	Answer	Mark
1 (a) (i)	N.E. England/the Ruhr	1
(ii)	**Either** N.E. England. Heavy industries, such as the iron and steel industry and shipbuilding grew up on Teesside and Tyneside respectively. The shipbuilding industry built ships for the export of coal. The chemical industry, specialising in synthetic fibres and the railway equipment industry grew up around Middlesborough and Stockton. **Or** The Ruhr. Its industries included the iron and steel industry, which produced steel that was used in the heavy electrical engineering industry and the armaments industry (at Essen), and the chemical and textile industries. The textile industry began producing woollen goods, then cotton and now largely synthetic fibres.	3
(iii)	**Either** N.E. England. Two industries selected – iron and steel and chemicals. The iron and steel industry developed aided by local coking coal and iron ore (from the Cleveland Hills). Later, iron ore was imported via the Tees estuary. There was local limestone and ample cooling water. Nearby, there were big markets in shipbuilding, railway works and the chemical industry. The chemical industry was favoured by the presence of local Teesside salt and anhydrite, sulphuric acid from the steelworks, coal for power and by-products, ample flat, cheap estuarine land, and more recently, oil piped in from the North Sea. **Or** The Ruhr. Two industries selected textiles and iron and steel. Factors favouring the textile industry included, in the early days of growth in the eighteenth and nineteenth century, local wool supplies; water and then coal for power; soft water for washing. Later, cotton began to be imported up the Rhine and a large prosperous local market grew up. Now synthetic oil based textiles are made using oil from the Wilhelmshaven pipeline, helped by cheap labour provided by the regions 'guest workers' e.g. Turks. The iron and steel industry aided by local coking coal and limestone. At first local ores, then ores imported up the Rhine and the Dortmund-Ems Canal. Huge local market in the region's heavy engineering, vehicle, chemical and textile industries.	6
(b) (i)	Most of the industry is of a sophisticated electronic nature reflecting the increasing wealth of the UK. Most of the products are for domestic and office use. This type of industry makes use of the regions improved road communications and employs more female labour than male, mostly semi-skilled.	3
(ii)	Such areas had high unemployment – so plenty of labour available and wage rates often lower than in S.E. England. Such areas attracted government grants and subsidies for they were 'Development Areas'.	4
(c)	In an LEDC many industries are of a primary type, e.g. mining and farming or are industries that do the early processes to the product mined or grown. The later stages of processing and marketing, where more money is made, are done in the MEDCs. However, in some LEDCs more	

Answers to Unit 9

Question	Answer	Mark
	sophisticated industry has developed e.g. in the 'Tiger' economies of S.E. Asia. In Brazil, for example, early industries were textiles and footwear in and around the state of São Paulo. These took advantage of: • locally grown cotton and leather from local cattle (raw materials); • cheap power from hydro-electricity generated on local rivers (energy); • rapid immigration meant that workers were cheap and plentiful (labour); • there was a poor, but large local population which needed the footwear and textile produced (market). As prosperity increased so industry became more advanced. The iron and steel industry grew up near Belo Horizonte helped by local iron ore, cheap electricity and manganese. More recently chemical, motor vehicle and engineering industries have developed in the states of Minas Gerais and São Paulo. These developments were helped by: • allowing foreign firms to set themselves up, thus tackling the problem of lack of worker skills and technical know-how (technology); • lack of capital meant Brazil needed to obtain loans from foreign countries, e.g. the USA. • larger loans from the World Bank helped improve communications (transport); • cheap electric power and the large home market still exists.	6

10 TOURISM AND LEISURE

Question	Answer	Mark
1 (a)		

Examiner's tip This question requires you to have a lot of specialised knowledge. The topics cover quite a range, so thorough revision is essential. In order to answer the question in full you need knowledge of the geography and climate of Europe and North Africa, some understanding of glacial and limestone landforms, a knowledge of National Parks and a complete understanding of the effects tourists have in National Parks and in developing countries as well as a detailed knowledge of winter tourism.

(i)

Examiner's tip Here you are asked to read a lot of information before attempting the question. Whilst reading each postcard carefully try to gain an impression of the type of holiday being described. The map you are given is not very detailed so think carefully before putting in your letters.

Answers to Unit 10

Question	Answer	Mark

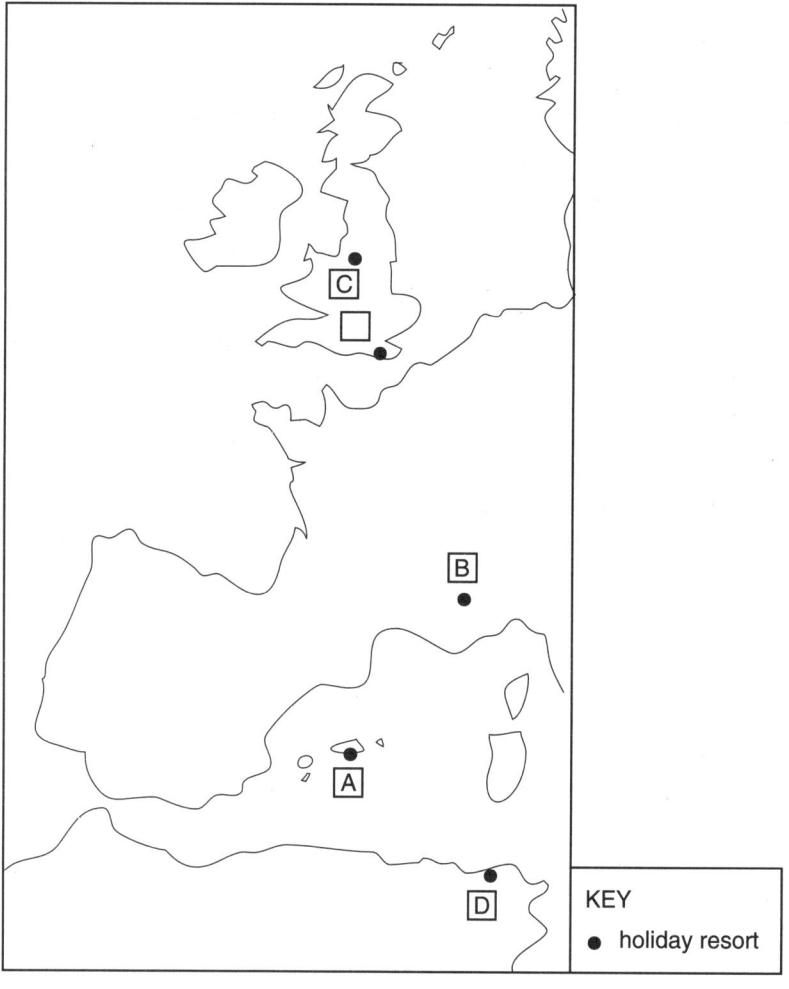

4

(ii)

Examiner's tip | Make sure you identify which of the two features you are describing.

A corrie is a feature of glacial erosion. It is an 'armchair'-like feature with steep back and side walls. Its open side faces a valley and there is sometimes a lake in the bottom of the corrie.

2

(iii) Pot-holes are a feature of limestone scenery as rainwater dissolves the rock removing it in solution. Soil does not form in limestone areas so bare grey-white rock outcrops are common.

2

(iv) National Parks were set up to protect and enhance areas of 'outstanding natural beauty'.

2

(v) Tourists may trample over farm land, leaving gates open, leaving litter behind and worrying farm animals. Noise and air pollution could disturb local residents and increased traffic could lead to congested roads, especially in summer.

2

Answers to Unit 10

Question	Answer	Mark
(vi)		

Examiner's tip You must name specific places in your answer, preferably ones you have studied in detail. Make sure you mention advantages as well as disadvantages.

In recent years many people have been attracted to Kenya for safari-type holidays. Kenyans have benefited through the creation of many jobs such as hotel staff, tour guides and drivers; tourists spending money in the local markets buying souvenirs; the money gained from touring big game reserves can go towards the upkeep and maintenance of animals. The disadvantages are that the money raised from tourism goes to tour operators or a few wealthy businessmen, it is not spread evenly throughout the country so not everyone benefits; tourists draw on limited local resources of water, electricity and fuel; local customs and traditions may suffer through the need to pamper tourists.

Upland farming areas of Britain, such as mid Wales, benefit from tourists in summer. Farming incomes are supplemented by providing bed and breakfast accommodation or selling local produce in farm shops and/or by offering guided walks and nature trails. The disadvantages are that tourists may trample on farmers' land, destroying crops and worrying animals, and that more tourists lead to congested roads and more litter. **6**

(b) The cold winter temperatures and adequate supply of precipitation provide excellent snow conditions attracting tourists for winter sports. Total precipitation is lower than many parts of the UK so the warm summers attract hikers and those who enjoy mountain scenery. **3**

(c)

Examiner's tip Study both the photograph and the diagram carefully. The key to the diagram can be most useful. Take special note of the direction of the north line. You must mention both natural and man-made attractions.

(i) Natural – It is a mountain environment with a plentiful supply of snow. Sunny days and clear blue skies make it ideal for skiing. There is a range of ski slopes catering for beginners and the more advanced skier. Ski runs are on north-facing slopes reducing the risk of snow melt.

Man-made – Many apartments and hotels have been built for accommodation. Facilities for children are provided, such as a crèche and a kindergarten, and ski hire and tuition. Prepared skiing areas (pistes) and a network of interconnecting ski lifts are available. **6**

(ii) The mountain environment is delicately balanced and thousands of visitors can upset sensitive plant and animal habitats. Removal of trees for ski runs leads to greater soil erosion in spring and increases the risk of avalanche in winter. The risk of flooding can increase as (i) bulldozing ski runs compacts the soil, reducing infiltration rates and (ii) tarmac car parking areas increase surface run-off. Small mountain streams can become raging torrents. **3**

Answers to Unit 11

11 EMPLOYMENT STRUCTURES IN DEVELOPED AND DEVELOPING COUNTRIES (MEDCs AND LEDCs)

Question	Answer	Mark
1 (a) (i)	1. The primary sector contains those industries which extract products from the Earth's surface. 2. The secondary sector is made up of industries in which raw materials are used to create something that people want.	2
(ii)	**Examiner's tip** You will need to examine these pie charts closely because some of the countries in the table have similar employment structures. 1 = United Kingdom 2 = Brazil	2
(iii)	**Examiner's tip** Note that the two axes concern primary and tertiary only; so you are matching these two components up. Thus, in A countries 1 and 2 will have high primary (>50) and low tertiary (<50) percentages. A = India B = Brazil C = United Kingdom Ghana South Korea Australia	3
(iv)	Developing = A Developed = C N.I.C. = B	1
(v)	**Examiner's tip** A wide range of characteristics can be used to answer this question. Choose any two of the following examples. 1. High birth rate, lowering death rate so high net reproduction. 2. Low gross national product. *OR* Poorly developed communication network. Poorly established welfare and social services.	2
(b)	**Examiner's tip** Study the data provided very carefully. You are given a lot of information, some of which can be used directly when answering the subsequent questions.	

Answers to Unit 11

Question	Answer	Mark

(i)

Examiner's tip — Do not forget the shading when completing this bar graph.

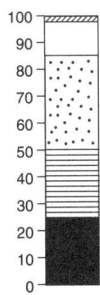

2

(ii) 1. Imports restricted   2. Cheap loans or tax incentives 2

(iii) Primary 1

(iv)

Examiner's tip — The changes you have to explain are the decline in the primary sector and the increases in the secondary and tertiary sectors. The chart provides you with strong clues for these changes but you are also expected to draw upon your own knowledge.

1. The introduction of machinery into mining and farming meant fewer workers were needed in the primary sector, forcing them to move into the secondary and tertiary sectors.
2. The government restricted imports forcing manufacturing to develop. *OR* Multinational (transnational) companies moved into the country with massive investment in the secondary sector.

4

(v) 1. Clothing is an essential, so there is a large home market in all developing countries for textiles.
2. The textile industry is fairly labour intensive. Labour in these countries is cheap. Thus costs of production are relatively low.
OR Most developing countries are tropical, so many grow cotton. This reduces costs.

4

(vi)

Examiner's tip — Note the use of the words 'economic' and 'social'. Economic relates to business and industry, social to people's well being, for example working hours, health and education.

Economic – Multinational companies may take their profits out of the country and invest them elsewhere.
OR The massive loans taken out to finance industrialisation may cripple the country's economy.

Social – Many employees have to work very long hours.
OR Urbanisation has led to growth of squatter settlements.

4

Answers to Unit 11

Question	Answer	Mark
(c)		

Examiner's tip This is a very open question. You can tackle industry or agriculture in any area of the developed or developing world. What you must do is specify the area and discuss decline.

Name of area: South-east Lancashire including what is now Greater Manchester.

(i) **Industry**. In the nineteenth century this was **the** most important **cotton textile** area in the world. It declined in the twentieth century because:

- Lancashire could no longer rely on cheap imports of raw cotton from developing countries.

- Lancashire could not compete with imports of cloth from developing countries, such as India, where overheads were much lower.

- Lancashire mills were slow to modernise their equipment.

- Synthetic fibres, such as nylon, reduced the market for cotton cloth.

(ii) There was a big rise in unemployment. This was very serious for male workers as there were few alternatives in an area where coal mining and heavy engineering were also in recession. There was a cumulative run down in facilities as people in the area had less and less money to spend. Many people moved away from the area in search of work. In some towns in the area, where employment for women still existed, they became the chief earners. **9**

2

Examiner's tip This is a scattergraph which shows the relationship between life expectancy and the percentage of the workforce employed in agriculture. Working in agriculture occupies the horizontal axis because it is thought to have an effect on life expectancy.

(a) The lower the percentage of the workforce employed in agriculture, the higher the life expectancy. **2**

(b) (i) If life expectancy is low, it suggests poor nutrition, poor medical services, high infant mortality and possibly people living in shanty towns; all indicative of a developing poor country.

(ii) As a country develops, so the percentage employed in agriculture declines. Agriculture becomes highly mechanised and employs less and less labour. So the lower the agricultural workforce percentage, the higher the stage of development. **4**

Answers to Unit 12

12 MOCK EXAMINATION PAPER

Question	Answer	Mark

1 (a)

Examiner's tip — Remember that on a 1:50000 scale map a grid square measures 2cm x 2cm, i.e. is 1 km × 1 km on the land and that this means the grid square has an area of 1 sq km.

    (i) 1 km   1

    (ii) 2 sq km   1

    (iii) So that tankers may moor and discharge their oil.   1

    (iv) Because the tankers are large and need deep water; the Haven has a deep channel close to the jetties.   2

(b)

Examiner's tip — Two marks are allocated in (iii) to the shading of Milford Haven, so be sure that you shade fully and accurately from Gelliswick Bay in the west to Castle Hall in the east. For the tanker route, (iv), be guided by the jetty positions.

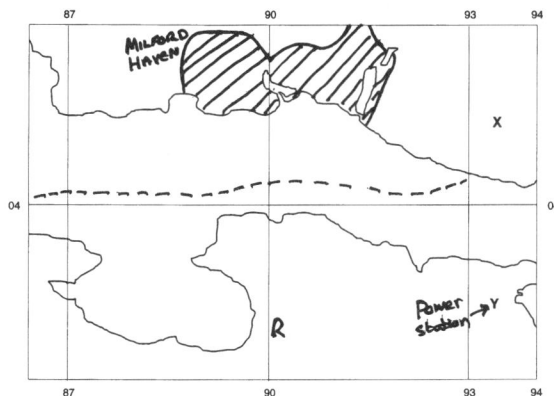

5

(c)

Examiner's tip — Study the contour lines on the OS map carefully.

    (i) The village is in a valley at the foot of a 40 metre slope. The refinery is at the top of it.   1

    (ii)

Examiner's tip — Though the question introduction does not insist that your information must come exclusively from the sources mentioned, there is sufficient in those sources to do so. As there are five marks available, five of the following statements will be sufficient. All the statements are directly or slightly indirectly derived from the sources provided.

They objected because there is a risk of explosions; the refineries can cause smells and fumes; air borne chemicals may damage objects not under cover as well as, possibly, people's health; these refineries are highly automated so not many of the unemployed will get jobs after they are built; they will spoil the scenery in a National Park; they will increase traffic on the roads; all this may reduce income from tourism.   5

Answers to Unit 12

Question	Answer	Mark

(iii) The Haven was wide enough for tankers to manoeuvre and deep enough to take their draught. There was ample, fairly level land near the coast for building. The Haven was sheltered from strong winds. — **3**

(d)

> **Examiner's tip** Make sure you tackle the three question sections: the pollution, its effect on the environment and the clean-up measures. You have a wide range of choice from oil spills, to chemical pollution of rivers or the air, to nuclear leakages. The Chernobyl disaster is chosen here.

In 1986 at Chernobyl the cooling system of a nuclear reactor failed. Fire broke out and a large mass of radioactive gas rose into the atmosphere. Because of upper air winds it spread out over much of North West Europe, including the UK, and some of the radioactivity was carried down to the ground by rain.

Its effects were widespread and long lasting. Not many people were killed in the explosion but many died subsequently from the effects of radioactivity. There were also malformed births in the Ukraine. In many places the vegetation was contaminated so milk sales were stopped in Germany; reindeer could not be used as meat in Lappland. Even in the UK in areas with heavy rainfall such as the Lake District and Wales, lambs were prevented from entering the food chain.

Unlike oil spills not too much can be done to clean up this type of pollution. It takes a long time to fade away. The reactor was capped with thick concrete to prevent further radioactivity. 10 cms of top soil was removed from farmland in the immediate vicinity of the plant. Damaging effects were reduced through slaughtering those animals worst affected. Other animals and grasses were monitored until radioactivity had dwindled away. The measures taken were as successful as could be hoped for. Total success is impossible for the consequences of radioactivity may be passed from generation to generation. — **6**

2 (a) (i)

> **Examiner's tip** When you look at the map you will see that there are works and docks and road and rail networks on either side of the estuary.

Many people live or work on both sides of the estuary. To cross it they have to travel inland to the bridging point.

Extra: People would meet at this bridging point and services would develop to cater for them. — **1**

(ii)

> **Examiner's tip** Note that though there are two marks for this question you must give four types of work.

Work in shops, offices, finance (such as banks and building societies), and entertainment (such as cinemas) are characteristic of the CBD. — **2**

(iii)

> **Examiner's tip** You probably will know quite a lot about this topic, but don't go into too much detail for there are only two marks to gain.

Answers to Unit 12

Question	Answer	Mark

1 Activities that need lots of workers and customers, such as shops, will set up business here because this is where the roads and railways converge, meeting at the most accessible point in the town.

2 Because land in this area is wanted by so many the value of land rises. It becomes too dear to live in and private houses are replaced by businesses.

2

(b)

Examiner's tip Obviously you must heed the either/or command. Do not be tempted to do both, however well you know the topics. You must use your time positively.

(i) **Either**

Examiner's tip This is a heavy engineering works. Its products are likely to be not only heavy but bulky. There are three marks available so make three points.

1 The land is likely to be flat at the side of an estuary so would be suitable for the work's layout.

2 This site is away from the CBD so land was probably cheap.

3 The docks were close by for export and import by water as was the railway for transport inland. These modes of transport are best for the bulky products of this works.

Extra: The works is close to the town for its labour supply.

3

Or

Examiner's tip These are light modern industries. They tend to transport their products by road.

1 The location of these factories close to the motorways is very suitable because these factory products are transported by lorry and truck to a wide range of often small markets.

2 Being built towards the edge of the town is advantageous to these firms because there is less traffic congestion here than nearer the town centre.

3 The land is cheaper so building costs were lower and there is room for expansion.

Extra: These factories are very accessible for their workers.

3

(c)

Examiner's tip Think about the changes in shopping habits and practices that have occurred during the past twenty-five years or so. These include the use of the car for transport of goods; use of freezers; the creation of large stores that can bulk buy and sell cheaper.

(i) These sites attract car owning customers because they are easily reached as they are at the junctions of major roads and often sell cheaper petrol. The stores can be large and laid out on one level for land is relatively cheap. There is plenty of room for large car parks which can be free for customers.

3

Answers to Unit 12

Question	Answer	Mark

(ii)

Examiner's tip — The question uses the word 'discuss'. This word is not often used at GCSE level. It suggests that you describe and explain and give both sides of the argument. There are five marks available here so some depth of answer is warranted.

These retail parks are posing a threat to CBD shopping areas because the public only has so much to spend and what they spend in these retail parks is no longer spent in town centres. These retail parks are convenient to the car owning, 'better off' section of the public because they are easily reached and have free parking, unlike the expensive multi-storey town centre ones. The CBD shopping area still has big advantages. There is a wider range of shops. Most specialist shops are here and there is an attractive support infrastructure of entertainment, restaurants, museums, libraries etc. Again, non-car owning people find this area easier to reach by public transport than retail parks. Possibly both types of shopping area will co-exist in the future.

5

(d)

Examiner's tip — Though not absolutely necessary in this case, because the circle is divided into sections of 25%, it is always advisable to take a protractor into a geography exam. Here tackle the easier ones 48% (just under half) and 23% (just under a quarter) first. The harder 29% has then been done automatically.

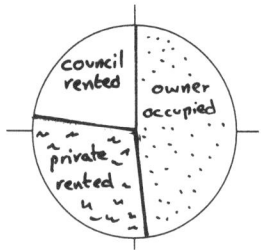

2

(ii)

Examiner's tip — There is an award of one mark only. So no great depth of answer is needed.

I think it is ward C. This ward is out in the suburbs. Here housing is of a higher standard. People often retire to these areas. OR This area has a low unemployment percentage. A high percentage of over 65s will help keep this low since they cannot be registered as unemployed.

1

(iii)

Examiner's tip — This question is about quality of life. Do not confuse this with standards of living, though normally you must have a reasonable standard of living to enjoy a good quality of life. Standard of living is measured by objective criteria such as quality of housing, intake of food, material possessions. But quality of life is harder to define. It varies with the individual. Two people with the same standard of living may have different qualities of life, because what they want from their surroundings differs. You can argue a case for any one of the wards but don't be too imaginative. The question states 'using the information given' so your answer must be based on evidence from the map and the statistical table

Answers to Unit 12

Question	Answer	Mark

Examiner's tip Two approaches are given below to show that there is more than one correct approach.

The quality of life, I think, is highest in Ward C. The table shows that nearly all its households are able to afford a car, so they are likely to be reasonably well off. The map shows that they are able to drive quickly onto the motorway and there are main roads into the town centre. Most the population own, or are buying, their homes. As this ward is near the edge of the city the houses are likely to be modern with gardens and close to the countryside. It is a pity that there is an industrial estate close to the ward but it is on the other side of the motorway and not likely to increase traffic on the ward's roads. Those people in the ward who work in the industrial estate haven't very far to travel so do not waste their time commuting. Most of the population enjoys this good quality of life for only 6% are unemployed.

(If I were a member of an ethnic minority). The quality of life I think would be best is in Ward A. There would be lots of people of my own kind around me, some of them relatives. We could share interests, help each other and keep our culture alive. Most of us would be in work and would own or be buying our homes. These would not cost too much as they are near the city centre, but they would be modernised and comfortable. It would not bother us too much if we didn't have a car because we are close to everything – shops, entertainment and the bus and train stations. There is public transport to take us all over the town and those working in the CBD can walk to work. There are corner shops to walk to for our everyday needs. This would be a good quality of life for me. I would enjoy it. **6**

---

3 (a)

Examiner's tip Make sure you read the correct block.

(i) China **1**

(ii) Oceania **1**

(iii) One of the following will be sufficient
Population figures are notoriously difficult to predict due to the difficulty in gaining accurate data.
Extras: Unpredictable fertility rates, unpredictable changes in economic status; the effectiveness of government/UN measures to reduce population growth in LEDCs and the impact of contraception information all make accurate predictions difficult. **2**

(b)

Examiner's tip This question assumes that you know which part of the world is classed as 'developing'. The four graphs you need to look at are Latin America, Africa, India and Other Asia.

(i) Share of world population is predicted to rise. **1**

(ii) Countries in the developing world are characterised as having a greater desire for large families; a lack of access to family planning information and contraception; having generally high birth rate at the present time and falling death rates. All or some of these will lead to an increase in population.

Answers to Unit 12

Question	Answer	Mark

Extra: Strong religious and cultural beliefs that discourage family planning. **3**

(iii) A rapidly rising population can lead to a lack of food and water; general poverty with a lack of adequate housing; people; uncontrolled urbanisation leading to congested mega-cities. Depletion of forests and associated environmental problems – drought and soil erosion.
Extras: Disease. Civil unrest. **3**

(iv) Note the question states 'international community' so specific local solutions are not required.
Measures could include: sharing of wealth so poverty levels are reduced; improving the social status of women which could include providing information and access to family planning; raising literacy rates – making sure that all children can read and write.
Extras: health care schemes; reducing spending on armaments; support long term aid schemes; MEDCs should recognise that it is a global problem and they too have a responsibility to commit an agreed percentage GDP. **4**

(c)

> **Examiner's tip** Again, it is assumed you know what is meant by the 'developed' world. Look at the graphs for North America, Europe and USSR/CIS.

(i) Decreasing **1**

(ii) Family planning readily available and is used more which allows women to work and pursue a career. Children are expensive and more people are materialistic desiring luxuries.
High standards of health care and high educational standards mean that more children grow up healthily and use their talents to the full. **2**

(iii)

> **Examiner's tip** This question relates to the problems of an increasingly aged population.

If a high percentage of the population are elderly then this puts strain on the welfare state – greater demands are placed on health care provision, social services need to provide more home helps, meals-on-wheels etc., more has to be paid out in state pensions.

Fewer young people means that there may be a shortage of labour – lack of skills, fewer workers in the 'active' age groups contribute less to welfare state in taxes and indirect contributions, etc. less money in the pot. Fewer people generally means fewer services - this may affect the elderly even more. **3**

(iv) During the 1950s Europe was able to support a high population density because an equable climate, relatively flat land and good, fertile soils meant that agriculture could produce sufficient food for the population. Industrialisation had meant that mineral reserves were developed generating a high degree of affluence. This money could be spent improving the overall quality of life by developing health schemes and raising educational standards. Trade with the rest of the world also generated income. **4**